Stop Overthinking

Your Comprehensive Guide to Developing Your Awareness, Learning CBT Techniques, and Embracing Daily Practices to Calm Your Anxiety and Worried Brain

Erica May

any other individual or persons for any purpose other than that for which it was initially intended. It is strictly prohibited to amend, reproduce, distribute, utilize, quote, or paraphrase any part of the content within this publication without prior authorization from the writer or publisher. Any violation of these regulations may result in legal action against those who have breached them.

Disclaimer Notice

The presented work is strictly informational and should not be interpreted as an offer to buy or sell any form of security, instrument, or investment vehicle. Furthermore, the information contained herein should not be taken as a medical, legal, tax, accounting, or investment recommendation given by the author(s) or any affiliated company, employees, or paid contributors. In other words, the information is presented without considering individual preferences for specific investments regarding risk parameters. General information does not account for a person's lifestyle and financial objectives. It is important to note that no tailored advice will be provided based on the given information.

Table of Contents

CHAPTER 6: STRUCTURED THINKING FOR UNSTRUCTURED MINDS

Harness the Power of Structured Thinking

Structured Problem-solving Techniques

Pathway to Clarity: A Structured Problem-Solving Process

CHAPTER 7: JOURNALING THE JUMBLED THOUGHTS

Harness the Power of Pen and Paper to Soothe Your Mind

Welcome to the

Ideas Worth Sharing

Series

My name is Nicholas Bright, and I've spent nearly two decades working as a psychologist specializing in Behavioral Neuroscience and Interpersonal Communication in the US, UK, and Australia. Throughout my career, I've encountered countless stories, experiences, and insights that have shaped my understanding of the human mind and interpersonal interactions.

This series is a collaborative effort, bringing together the experience and expertise of myself and my colleagues: Erica May, Jeff Sharpe, Camila Alvarez, and potentially new faces in the future! We've chosen to write under pen names to respect everyone's privacy and keep the spotlight on the valuable content we offer rather than us as individuals. This decision allows us to freely share our knowledge without the distractions that often come with the limelight. We stand by the authenticity and credibility of the content shared here—our professional integrity remains at the forefront of this series.

We are deeply passionate about our field, and our primary goal is to equip you with practical, research-backed insights that you can implement in your everyday life. Each chapter is designed to inspire and help you better understand yourself and those around you.

We invite you to engage actively with the material: take notes, discuss the ideas with friends and family, and, most importantly, apply the lessons in your daily routine.

1. **Read;** understand what can be done to improve
2. **Reflect;** appreciate your feelings and their origins
3. **Remember;** put your learning into action

Thank you for embarking on this journey of knowledge and growth with us,

Nick

Want to Win Free Books?

Join Our Newsletter!

In this series, we appreciate that someone may find many different books helpful. I certainly know that when discussing sensitive topics like, for example, divorce, we can end up working on grief, anxiety, self-confidence, cognitive dissonance, and lots more. When we encounter a major challenge in life, it is rarely due to one small problem but rather a concoction of our experiences, outlooks, and actions; it's often a deep-rooted issue with many different things we need to uncover and support. We are complicated beings, and we must recognize this. As such, I would love to invite you all to join our newsletter.

In this, I aim to write articles of interest, including excerpts from various books in the series, as well as **vouchers**, **discounts**, and **giveaways**—and of course, no gimmicks or catches. I harbor a deep loathing of companies that offer seemingly amazing deals, only to charge you vast amounts in hidden fees! I vowed to never fall into that trap myself, and any offers I make are designed to be of true benefit and help. If you win a book in a giveaway, I want you to read it with a smile.

Join our newsletter and discover the additional value we can add to your life's curriculum!

Join us at: **www.IdeasWorthSharingSeries.com/newsletter**

See you on the inside!

About the Author: Dr. Erica May

Dr Erica May is a dedicated Clinical Psychologist practising in New York City. She graduated from Syracuse University in New York State, earning her degree in Clinical Psychology. Erica specializes in Cognitive Behavioral Therapy (CBT), Dialectical Behavior Therapy (DBT), and trauma-focused treatments. Her work is deeply rooted in helping individuals navigate complex emotional landscapes, enabling them to lead healthier and more fulfilling lives. Her compassionate approach and expertise have garnered her a reputation as a trusted mental health professional in her local community.

Erica has been friends and has worked with Nicholas Bright, the lead author of the Ideas Worth Sharing series, for many years. Together, they aim to help support a wider community by writing a book series on important topics within Psychology and extending their therapeutic insights and techniques beyond the confines of their practice. This book series will cover various topics related to mental health, including detailed guides on implementing CBT and DBT strategies in daily life, as well as comprehensive approaches to prevention, understanding and healing. By presenting practical exercises and learning through her practice, Erica hopes to make evidence-based psychological concepts more accessible to a broader audience. She aims to empower individuals with the knowledge and tools to manage their mental health proactively and independently, fostering greater resilience and well-being.

Preface

"He who conquers himself is the mightiest warrior."

Confucius

In the clamor of our everyday lives, where thoughts often become turbulent whirlwinds, finding clarity can seem like an elusive quest. This book is born from recognizing that struggle, offering a beacon of hope and practical strategies to those frequently ensnared by their own thoughts. The essence of this guide is simple yet profound: to equip you with the tools necessary to master your mind, embrace calm, and leave overthinking and anxiety behind.

Drawing from a rich tapestry of cognitive-behavioral techniques and mindfulness practices, this book delves into what causes us to overthink and how to stop it. It's designed to educate and transform, aiming to shift your mental habits from chaotic to controlled, from anxious to serene.

The journey of crafting this book was not solitary. It was shaped by conversations with psychologists, feedback from early readers who resonated deeply with the preliminary drafts, and countless hours of research that ensured the integrity and effectiveness of the advice given. I am profoundly grateful to all who contributed by offering insights or sharing your stories.

To my readers, thank you for choosing to embark on this journey with me. You have taken a courageous step towards reclaiming your inner peace and mental clarity. This book is for anyone who feels overwhelmed by their thoughts—a professional struggling with decision fatigue, a student anxious about future prospects, or anyone in between. No specific expertise is required; it is a willingness to engage openly with the practices outlined.

As you turn these pages, I invite you to actively engage with each strategy and envision a life where you are no longer at the mercy of your racing thoughts but are empowered to lead a calmer, more fulfilling life. Thank you for your trust and commitment. Let's begin this transformative journey together and unlock the serene mind that awaits beyond the pages.

Introduction

"The only way to make sense out of change is

to plunge into it, move with it,

and join the dance."

Alan Watts

The constant barrage of information and demands in our fast-paced world can often lead to overwhelming thoughts and feelings. People commonly find themselves trapped in a cycle of overthinking, where their thoughts seem to endlessly loop without resolution. This incessant thinking can cloud judgment, impede decision-making, and create a state of chronic anxiety. Recognizing the profound impact of these mental patterns on one's overall quality of life is the first step toward seeking change.

This book is written with the understanding that overthinking is not just a minor inconvenience but a pervasive issue that can affect all areas of life. Whether you're struggling to make decisions, feeling paralyzed by worry, or constantly replaying past mistakes, the insights and strategies covered within these pages aim to provide you with the tools needed to break free from this pattern. The journey towards mental clarity is one of self-discovery and empowerment.

Throughout the chapters, we'll delve deep into the mechanisms of overthinking. Understanding how and why your mind engages in these patterns is crucial for developing strategies to counteract them. By identifying the triggers and root causes of overthinking, you can begin to address the issue at its core rather than merely treating its symptoms. This foundational knowledge sets the stage for the following practical techniques and exercises.

Cognitive-behavioral techniques form a significant part of our discussion. These methods have been extensively studied and proven effective in reshaping thought patterns and behaviors. By learning to reframe negative thoughts and challenge irrational beliefs, you can gradually train your mind to adopt a more balanced and realistic perspective. The book provides actionable steps to integrate these techniques into daily life, ensuring they become second nature over time.

Mindfulness practices are another cornerstone of this guide. The ability to stay present and fully engage with the current moment can significantly reduce the tendency to overthink. Mindfulness helps manage stress and fosters a deeper connection with oneself and the world. Practical exercises and meditations are included to help cultivate this valuable skill, lending to a more centered and peaceful state of being.

In addition to cognitive-behavioral and mindfulness strategies, we explore the importance of narrative. Personal stories and relatable anecdotes are woven throughout the chapters to illustrate the concepts discussed. These narratives make the content more engaging and demonstrate the real-world application of the techniques, making them more tangible and relatable.

The book is designed to be personalized and adaptable. You are encouraged to reflect on your experiences and apply the strategies that resonate with your unique circumstances. This isn't a one-size-fits-all solution; it's a toolkit that can be tailored to your needs. The exercises and reflections provided are meant to be interactive, prompting you to engage deeply and make the practices your own.

It's also important to acknowledge that the journey to overcoming overthinking is not a linear one. Progress may come in waves, with periods of clarity interspersed with challenges. The key is to remain persistent and compassionate with yourself, recognizing that change takes time and effort. You can achieve lasting transformation by consistently applying the strategies and being patient with your progression.

The insights and techniques shared in this book aim to empower you to take control of your thoughts and, by extension, your life. The goal is to move from a state of mental clutter and anxiety to one of clarity, calm, and purpose. The process requires commitment, but the rewards are profound—a life where you are no longer held back by overthinking but instead free to fully engage with the richness of your existence.

Chapter 1: The Overthinking Odyssey

"Mindfulness isn't difficult. We just need to

remember to do it."

Sharon Salzberg

Is Your Mind Running in Circles?

Imagine your mind as a tool—designed to think, process, and resolve. But what happens when this tool becomes a trap, ensnaring you in a relentless loop of thoughts that lead nowhere? This is the heart of overthinking—a mental habit distinguishing itself sharply from the beneficial act of reflective thinking. While the latter propels you forward, the former tends to pull you back or freeze you in place. Our journey through this chapter will arm you with an understanding of how to differentiate these processes and regain control over your mental narrative.

Overthinking is not just a personal inconvenience; it's a pervasive issue that affects millions, influencing their professional achievements and personal relationships. It can transform a regular decision-making process into an agonizing ordeal and convert momentary worries into endless sources of stress. Here, we'll explore how this form of thinking can become detrimental and the psychological impacts it carries. By recognizing these effects, readers can begin to understand the severity of unchecked thought patterns on both personal growth and professional performance.

Understanding the Triggers is crucial. Overthinking doesn't arise in a vacuum—it's often triggered by specific events or environments. Identifying these triggers is the first step toward disarming them. We will delve into common patterns that precipitate overthinking, helping you to recognize and address these catalysts proactively.

This chapter also sets the stage for what lies ahead in Thought Breakers: Unlocking Mental Clarity. You'll see how chronic overthinking not only hampers your immediate well-being but also how it fits into larger patterns of anxiety and stress that can dominate your life. The strategies discussed here are band-aid solutions and long-term approaches to cultivating mental clarity.

The tools we introduce are grounded in cognitive-behavioral techniques and mindfulness practices—approaches celebrated for their effectiveness in transforming thought patterns and reducing anxiety. These practical strategies can be seamlessly integrated into daily routines, ensuring they are accessible regardless of lifestyle or starting point.

Take Control of Your Thoughts.

As we progress, remember that overcoming overthinking is highly personal. The techniques provided are flexible enough to be tailored to individual needs and situations, empowering you to build a personalized toolkit for mental clarity.

By the end of this text, our goal is clear: equip you with the knowledge to deeply understand your thought processes and provide actionable steps that significantly reduce overthinking. This isn't just about coping—it's about thriving. Through mastery over your thoughts, you can unlock levels of productivity and personal satisfaction that have been dampened by incessant overthinking.

The Crucial Difference Between Reflective Thinking and Overthinking

Reflective thinking and overthinking are two mental processes that may seem similar at first glance but have vastly different outcomes. Reflective thinking involves purposeful contemplation on a specific issue or situation, aiming to gain insight, learn from past experiences, and make informed decisions. It is a valuable tool for personal growth and problem-solving. On the other hand, overthinking is a detrimental mental habit characterized by a continuous loop of repetitive thoughts that often lead to no resolution or insight.

Reflective thinking is about learning and growing, while overthinking is about getting stuck in a cycle of unproductive thoughts. When reflecting, individuals consider various perspectives, analyze information, and draw conclusions to move forward. In contrast, overthinkers find themselves trapped in a web of endless contemplation, unable to break free from the grip of their own minds.

One key distinction between reflective thinking and overthinking is their impact on mental well-being. Reflective thinking typically results in increased self-awareness and improved decision-making skills. In contrast, overthinking can lead to heightened anxiety, indecision, and mental exhaustion. This constant rumination on negative scenarios or past events can create unnecessary stress and hinder progress.

Recognizing the difference between reflective thinking and overthinking is crucial for breaking free from the cycle of excessive contemplation. By acknowledging when one has crossed the line from productive reflection to unproductive overanalysis, individuals can take steps to redirect their thought patterns toward more constructive pathways. Developing self-awareness around these mental processes is the first step towards regaining control over one's thoughts and emotions.

Individuals can cultivate a healthier relationship with their thoughts by understanding the distinction between reflective thinking and overthinking. It's essential to recognize when contemplation becomes an endless loop of unproductive rumination and take proactive steps to shift towards more purposeful reflection.

Overthinking can have profound psychological impacts on both personal and professional life, creating a cycle of anxiety and stress that can be challenging to break. In personal relationships, overthinking can lead to misinterpretations, misunderstandings, and unnecessary conflicts. This constant mental rumination can cause individuals to perceive slights where none exist, leading to a breakdown in communication and trust. Feelings of insecurity and self-doubt can be amplified through overthinking, making it difficult for individuals to maintain healthy and fulfilling relationships.

Professionally, overthinking can hinder decision-making and problem-solving abilities. The continuous loop of thoughts can cloud judgment, leading to indecision or over-analysis of situations. This can result in missed opportunities, delayed progress, and increased stress in the workplace. Overthinking may also manifest as perfectionism, where individuals are never satisfied with their work due to excessive scrutiny and self-criticism.

Moreover, the cognitive load of constant overthinking can lead to mental exhaustion, impacting overall productivity and performance levels. Individuals may find it challenging to concentrate on tasks or make clear-headed decisions when their minds are preoccupied with excessive contemplation. This can create a vicious cycle where decreased productivity leads to heightened anxiety, further fueling the overthinking pattern.

Over time, chronic overthinking can take a toll on mental health, contributing to increased levels of anxiety, depression, and overall emotional distress. The inability to switch off the relentless stream of thoughts can lead to sleep disturbances, further exacerbating the negative impact on mental well-being. Individuals caught in this cycle may experience feelings of overwhelm and helplessness, unable to break free from the grip of overthinking.

Recognizing the detrimental effects of overthinking is crucial in taking steps toward breaking free from this harmful pattern. Acknowledging how overthinking impacts personal relationships and professional success, individuals can implement strategies promoting mental clarity and emotional well-being. Through practical techniques and a shift in mindset, it is possible to overcome the psychological impacts of overthinking and cultivate a more balanced approach to thought processes.

Understanding the profound consequences of overthinking is the first step towards reclaiming control over one's mental landscape. By recognizing the toll it takes on personal relationships, professional performance, and overall well-being, individuals can begin to unravel the patterns that keep them trapped in a cycle of anxiety and stress. Through targeted interventions and a commitment to change, it is possible to break free from overthinking and embrace a more mindful and purposeful way of engaging with the world.

Identifying the common triggers and patterns that lead to overthinking is crucial in breaking free from this detrimental mental habit. One prevalent trigger is perfectionism, where individuals set unrealistically high standards for themselves, leading to constant self-criticism and overanalyzing every detail. Recognizing the need for perfection and accepting that mistakes are a natural part of growth can help alleviate this pressure.

Another common trigger is rumination, where individuals repeatedly dwell on past events or conversations, often with a negative bias. This pattern can keep the mind stuck in a loop of unproductive thoughts, fostering anxiety and self-doubt. To combat rumination, it's essential to practice mindfulness and redirect the focus towards the present moment, allowing for a break from incessant overthinking.

External stressors like work deadlines, relationship issues, or financial concerns can fuel overthinking. When faced with overwhelming external pressures, individuals may be trapped in a cycle of worry and analysis paralysis. Setting boundaries, prioritizing tasks, and seeking support from friends, family, or professionals can help manage these stressors effectively.

Fear of the unknown is another significant trigger for overthinking. The uncertainty of future outcomes or decisions can lead to excessive planning and forecasting, creating a sense of constant unease. Practicing acceptance of uncertainty and focusing on what can be controlled in the present moment can alleviate the anxiety associated with the unknown.

Negative self-talk plays a crucial role in perpetuating overthinking patterns. When individuals engage in self-criticism and doubt their abilities or worth, they are more likely to spiral into overthinking loops. Challenging negative thoughts with positive affirmations, self-compassion, and cognitive restructuring techniques can help break this destructive cycle.

Perceived lack of control over situations can also trigger overthinking. When individuals feel helpless or unable to influence outcomes, they may resort to excessive mental processing as a way to regain a sense of control. Empowering oneself through taking small actionable steps towards goals, seeking guidance from mentors or therapists, and reframing challenges as opportunities for growth can shift this mindset.

Understanding these triggers and patterns that lead to overthinking is the first step towards regaining control over one's thoughts and emotions. By recognizing these common pitfalls and implementing practical strategies to address them, individuals can gradually break free from the cycle of excessive contemplation and move towards a more balanced and peaceful state of mind.

In this chapter, we've embarked on a critical exploration of the often misunderstood terrain of overthinking. We've drawn a distinct line between reflective thinking, which serves as a constructive tool, and detrimental overthinking, which spirals into a trap of unproductive mental loops. Understanding this distinction is crucial, laying the groundwork for healthier mental habits and improved decision-making.

Recognizing the profound impact of overthinking on your personal and professional life is the first step toward transformation. Appreciating how these mental patterns strain relationships, diminish work performance, and barricade personal growth and well-being is essential. You can better intercept these cycles before they escalate by identifying the common triggers and patterns that lead to overthinking.

Each chapter will build upon this foundation, providing practical strategies and actionable insights. These tools are designed to cope and thrive, transforming overthinking into an opportunity for personal development and clarity.

The journey through this book promises to be both enlightening and empowering. As you progress, you'll discover how mastering your mind is not just about reducing overthinking but about fostering a state of mental clarity that enhances every aspect of your life. You have the innate ability to redirect your mental energy from cyclical worries to constructive thoughts.

Embrace this opportunity to break free from the chains of overthinking. With each page turned you'll find yourself one step closer to a clearer, more serene mind and a more fulfilling life. Let's continue this journey together, equipped with knowledge and ready to reclaim the calmness and confidence that is rightfully yours.

Chapter 2: The Myth of the Analytical Mind

"We don't see things as they are,

we see them as we are."

Anaïs Nin

Unraveling the Tangled Web of Overthinking

Overthinking is often mistakenly glorified as a hallmark of intelligence and deep analytical prowess. Yet, this widespread belief obscures the more detrimental effects of excessive rumination on mental clarity and productivity. In an era where information overload is common, understanding the true impact of overthinking is crucial for anyone aiming to achieve mental clarity and effective decision-making.

The Misconception: Overthinking as an Intellectual Asset

Many assume that a highly analytical mind is constantly active, dissecting every detail and scenario. This characteristic is frequently celebrated and linked with high intelligence and thorough decision-making. However, this chapter will challenge this notion, arguing that overthinking may hinder rather than enhance our cognitive abilities. By exploring this misconception, we aim to shift the perspective from glorifying mental chatter to recognizing its traps.

Analysis Paralysis: The Real Cost of Overthinking

The phenomenon of analysis paralysis illustrates the practical drawbacks of overthinking. When individuals become trapped in their thoughts, endlessly weighing options and scenarios, they stall their ability to act. This section will delve into how analysis paralysis slows down productivity and contributes to increased stress and decreased overall well-being. Understanding this relationship is pivotal for those seeking to break free from the cycles of overanalysis.

Intelligence and Overthinking: Correlation or Confusion?

It is commonly believed that smarter individuals naturally think more — and more deeply — about everything. However, intelligence should empower action, not hinder it with incessant deliberation. This chapter will discuss the nuanced relationship between intelligence and overthinking, debunking myths that link them inherently and exploring how intelligent minds can cultivate decisiveness amidst a sea of thoughts.

By providing these insights, we pave the way for readers to recognize when thoughtful reflection crosses into counterproductive overthinking. The goal is not merely awareness but empowerment—equipping you with the knowledge to harness your intellectual energy efficiently without falling prey to its potential pitfalls.

Our approach throughout will emphasize practical strategies to mitigate overthinking. These include setting clear objectives, limiting decision-making time, and applying structured problem-solving techniques. Each strategy aims to reduce unnecessary mental clutter and enhance your decisiveness.

Understanding these dynamics is essential for anyone seeking mental clarity in their personal or professional life. By identifying the triggers and consequences of overthinking, you can begin to take control back from the incessant need to analyze every detail. This empowerment leads to a clearer, more focused state of mind that values quality of thought over quantity.

In embracing these concepts, you take an important step towards mastering your mental landscape—transforming potential mental barriers into effective living and decision-making tools. Remember, the goal is actionable intelligence, not just activity in thought.

Overthinking is often glamorized as a sign of intelligence and deep analytical prowess. Many believe that the more one thinks, the more one can uncover solutions and insights others might overlook. However, the reality is far from this romanticized view. Overthinking can be a double-edged sword, leading to a state of analysis paralysis where one gets trapped in endless loops of thoughts without making progress toward a resolution. This misconception about overthinking's benefits can hinder personal growth and productivity rather than enhancing it.

One common myth surrounding overthinking is that it leads to better decision-making. The belief is that by meticulously analyzing every aspect of a situation, one can arrive at the best possible outcome. However, in practice, excessive rumination can cloud judgment and create confusion rather than clarity. The constant churn of thoughts can make it challenging to discern essential information from noise, leading to indecision and procrastination.

Another misconception is that overthinkers are more creative or innovative, delving deep into problems to uncover unique solutions. While it's true that critical thinking plays a role in creativity, excessive overanalyzing can stifle the creative process.

Instead of exploring new possibilities, overthinkers may get bogged down in minute details, losing sight of the bigger picture and missing out on innovative ideas.

Overthinking is sometimes seen as preventing mistakes by considering all possible outcomes before taking action. However, this approach often backfires as the fear of making errors paralyzes individuals from moving forward. Perfectionism fueled by overthinking can lead to missed opportunities as the focus shifts from progress to avoiding failure at all costs.

Dispelling these common misconceptions about the benefits of overthinking is crucial for individuals looking to break free from its grip. Recognizing that overthinking does not necessarily equate to intelligence or superior problem-solving skills is the first step toward reclaiming mental clarity and emotional well-being. By understanding the pitfalls of excessive rumination, one can seek healthier ways to approach challenges and make decisions effectively.

Understanding Analysis Paralysis and Its Impact on Productivity

Overthinking often leads to a state known as analysis paralysis, where individuals find themselves trapped in a cycle of endless thoughts without taking decisive action. This condition hampers productivity, causing individuals to feel overwhelmed and unable to move forward effectively. Analysis paralysis can be particularly detrimental in work settings, where decisions must be made promptly, and actions must be taken efficiently. When overthinking takes over, making clear choices or completing tasks becomes challenging, leading to missed opportunities and decreased performance.

The effects of analysis paralysis ripple through various aspects of life, affecting not only work but also personal relationships and overall well-being. People caught in this cycle may struggle to make simple decisions, constantly second-guessing themselves and feeling uncertain about their choices. This indecisiveness can breed frustration, erode confidence, and lead to feelings of inadequacy. The inability to break free from analysis paralysis can create a self-perpetuating cycle of stress and anxiety, further exacerbating the problem.

Breaking free from analysis paralysis requires a shift in mindset and approach. Instead of getting lost in endless contemplation, it's essential to recognize when overthinking is hindering progress and take steps to refocus on action. Setting clear goals and priorities can help direct thoughts toward concrete outcomes, steering away from the unproductive loop of excessive rumination. Practicing mindfulness can also aid in staying present and centered, preventing the mind from spiraling into overthinking patterns.

Implementing time management techniques can be instrumental in combating analysis paralysis. By breaking tasks into smaller, manageable steps and setting deadlines for completion, individuals can prevent themselves from getting bogged down by excessive deliberation. Creating a supportive environment that encourages decisive action and provides feedback can also help overcome analysis paralysis. Surrounding oneself with positive influences and constructive feedback can boost confidence and alleviate the fear of making mistakes.

Recognizing the signs of analysis paralysis is crucial for regaining control over one's thoughts and actions. By acknowledging when overthinking is impeding progress and actively working towards breaking free from this pattern, individuals can reclaim their productivity and focus on achieving their goals effectively. Remember, action is the antidote to analysis paralysis, so take deliberate steps towards breaking free from the shackles of endless contemplation and embrace a more purposeful way of living.

Discussing the Link Between Intelligence and Overthinking

When exploring the intricate relationship between intelligence and overthinking, it is crucial to debunk the myth that overthinking is a direct indicator of high intelligence. While intelligence can contribute to deep analytical thinking, overthinking often deviates from productive analysis into a state of rumination. Intelligence, in its essence, involves the ability to process information efficiently, make sound decisions, and solve problems effectively. Overthinking, on the other hand, tends to hinder these processes by trapping individuals in a cycle of endless thoughts that lead to indecision and inaction.

It's important to recognize that intelligence manifests in various forms, including emotional intelligence, creative thinking, and practical problem-solving skills. Overthinking does not necessarily align with these manifestations; instead, it clouds judgment and impedes clear decision-making. Therefore, it's essential to distinguish between deep contemplation driven by intelligence and overthinking characterized by excessive worry and doubt.

Overthinking can hinder cognitive abilities, draining mental energy that could be utilized for more constructive purposes. The constant churn of thoughts associated with overthinking can lead to mental fatigue, decreased focus, and impaired cognitive function. In contrast, true intelligence empowers individuals to think critically, adapt to challenges, and find effective solutions without getting entangled in unproductive thought loops.

To break free from the cycle of overthinking, individuals must cultivate self-awareness to recognize when their thoughts veer into unproductive territory. Developing mindfulness practices can help enhance clarity of mind and promote a more balanced approach to problem-solving. By acknowledging the limitations of overthinking and embracing the strengths of true intelligence, individuals can navigate challenges with greater ease and efficiency.

Ultimately, intelligence shines through not in the complexity of one's thoughts but in the clarity and effectiveness of one's actions. By understanding the distinction between deep analysis rooted in intelligence and counterproductive overthinking, individuals can harness their mental faculties more efficiently and lead a more fulfilling life marked by thoughtful decision-making rather than endless rumination.

In exploring our minds, it's crucial to dismantle the myths that bind us to counterproductive habits. Overthinking, often misinterpreted as a sign of profound analytical prowess, impedes our ability to think clearly and act decisively. By understanding the true impacts of this habit, we can begin to free ourselves from its grip.

Dispelling the myths surrounding overthinking is a vital first step. It's easy to assume that constant rumination leads to better decisions, but this is seldom true. Instead, it typically results in analysis paralysis, where decision-making stalls and stress accumulates. Recognizing this can be both liberating and empowering.

The link between intelligence and overthinking is also frequently misunderstood. High intelligence does not necessitate a tendency to overthink; rather, it should empower us to make efficient, effective decisions. By reevaluating how we perceive intelligence, we encourage a healthier mental approach that values clarity and purpose over unnecessary complexity.

To truly master our mental processes, embracing strategies that promote decisiveness and emotional resilience is essential. Simple, actionable steps such as setting clear goals, practicing mindfulness, and limiting the time spent on decision-making can profoundly alter our mental landscape. These practices not only enhance productivity but also improve our overall mental well-being.

We reclaim control over our mental space by actively engaging with these strategies. This shift allows us to move from passive overthinkers to active, mindful participants, leading to greater satisfaction and effectiveness in our personal and professional endeavors.

As we move forward, let's carry with us the understanding that overthinking is not an asset but a hindrance that can be overcome. With the right tools and a shift in perspective, achieving mental clarity and emotional balance is within reach for everyone.

Chapter 3: The Anxiety-Overthinking Nexus

"The present moment is the only time

over which we have dominion."

Thích Nhất Hạnh

Trapped in Your Own Mind? Discover the Path to Mental Clarity

When thoughts swirl chaotically, it's like being stuck in a relentless storm. Understanding the intricate dance between overthinking and anxiety is crucial for those seeking relief from this mental tempest. This chapter will delve into how persistent overthinking not only fuels anxiety but can also lock individuals in a vicious cycle that impacts overall mental health and well-being.

Overthinking involves repeatedly analyzing situations beyond their importance, often leading to indecision, procrastination, and heightened stress. It's a common misconception that overthinking aids in finding better solutions; however, it typically exacerbates feelings of unease and uncertainty. By exploring this relationship, we aim to give you knowledge and strategies to break free from these mental shackles.

Anxiety, a natural response to perceived threats, can become overwhelming when continuously triggered by overthinking. This state of constant alertness can drain your emotional reservoirs significantly. We'll examine how this cycle of anxiety is perpetuated by overthinking and discuss ways to interrupt this pattern effectively.

Chronic overthinkers often do not realize the toll their habits take on their mental health until significant symptoms manifest. These may include sleep disturbances, inability to concentrate, and even physical symptoms such as headaches or digestive issues. Acknowledging these effects is the first step towards recovery.

Strategies for Breaking the Cycle

To address these challenges, this chapter introduces practical techniques designed to reduce overthinking and alleviate anxiety. These include mindfulness exercises, cognitive restructuring methods, and establishing a routine encouraging mental breaks and healthy thought patterns.

Empowering yourself begins with understanding the triggers of your overthinking. By becoming aware of these triggers, you can develop proactive strategies to manage them before they escalate into full-blown anxiety. This proactive approach enhances your coping ability and improves your overall quality of life.

The journey towards mental clarity is not about suppressing thoughts but managing them constructively. Our goal is to guide you through reshaping your thinking patterns and adopting new behaviors that foster peace and stability in your mind.

By embracing these strategies, you are taking control of your mental landscape. Remember, mastering your mind is a skill that can be developed like any other—a journey of self-discovery and resilience paving the way to a calmer, more fulfilling life.

Chronic overthinkers often find themselves caught in a cycle of heightened anxiety, where their minds continuously churn through thoughts and scenarios, leading to increased stress levels. The relationship between overthinking and anxiety is closely intertwined, with one feeding into the other in a never-ending loop. Overthinking tends to magnify perceived threats and challenges, triggering the body's stress response, which, in turn, fuels more overthinking as the mind attempts to find solutions or predict outcomes.

As individuals engage in repetitive analysis and rumination, they inadvertently elevate their anxiety levels. Constantly reevaluating decisions and interactions can lead to perpetual worry, where even minor issues become amplified in the mind. This heightened alertness can exhaust mental resources, leaving individuals feeling drained and overwhelmed by their thoughts. The more one dwells on potential problems or uncertainties, the more anxious they are likely to become.

Moreover, the overthinking-anxiety nexus can create a sense of paralysis, where individuals struggle to make decisions or take action due to fear of making the wrong choice. This indecisiveness further fuels anxiety as individuals become trapped in a cycle of analyzing every possible outcome and consequence. The fear of making mistakes or facing negative outcomes can be paralyzing, preventing individuals from moving forward and perpetuating feelings of anxiety and stress.

Recognizing this harmful cycle and understanding that overthinking is not a productive problem-solving strategy is essential. While reflection and consideration are valuable, excessive rumination can lead to heightened anxiety and hinder decision-making abilities. Learning to manage overthinking can significantly reduce anxiety levels and improve overall well-being.

Persistent overthinking can trigger a cycle of anxiety that can be difficult to break. When thoughts become obsessive and intrusive, they fuel feelings of worry and apprehension, leading to heightened stress levels. This constant mental churn can create a loop where anxiety feeds into overthinking, which in turn fuels more anxiety, creating a vicious cycle that can be challenging to escape.

One key aspect of this cycle is the tendency to catastrophize. Overthinkers often magnify potential negative outcomes in their minds, imagining the worst-case scenarios of a situation. This catastrophizing mindset can intensify feelings of anxiety, making it hard to see things clearly or rationally. As a result, the overthinker becomes trapped in a cycle of fear and worry, unable to break free from the grip of their anxious thoughts.

Another element that perpetuates this cycle is the need for certainty. Overthinkers often seek reassurance and guarantees in every decision, constantly second-guessing themselves to avoid possible mistakes. However, this quest for certainty only fuels overthinking and anxiety, as life inherently comes with uncertainties that cannot always be controlled or predicted. This relentless pursuit of certainty can lead to paralysis and indecision, further exacerbating anxiety levels.

The constant analysis and reanalysis of past events and conversations also play a significant role in perpetuating the anxiety-overthinking cycle. Overthinkers dwell on past interactions, dissecting every word and gesture and searching for hidden meanings or potential pitfalls. This rumination on the past keeps them stuck in a loop of self-doubt and anxiety, preventing them from moving forward with confidence.

Breaking free from this cycle requires conscious effort and self-awareness. Recognizing when overthinking leads to increased anxiety is the first step towards regaining control over one's thoughts and emotions. Practicing mindfulness can help individuals become more aware of their thought patterns and learn to observe them without judgment or attachment. Setting boundaries around excessive rumination and implementing strategies like journaling, deep breathing exercises, or progressive muscle relaxation can also help interrupt the cycle of anxiety fueled by overthinking.

By understanding the intricate relationship between overthinking and heightened anxiety, individuals can begin to dismantle this harmful cycle. Empowering oneself with tools and techniques to manage both overthinking tendencies and anxiety symptoms is crucial for breaking free from this detrimental pattern. Through consistent practice and self-reflection, it is possible to gradually reduce anxiety levels and regain a sense of mental clarity and peace.

Chronic overthinking can have profound long-term effects on mental health, leading to a range of issues that impact overall well-being. Repetitive overanalysis and constant rumination can wear down the mind, increasing stress levels and anxiety. This continuous cycle of overthinking can result in mental exhaustion, making it challenging to focus, make decisions, or find peace of mind. Over time, this can manifest as various mental health conditions, such as generalized anxiety disorder, depression, or even panic attacks.

The prolonged exposure to high-stress levels due to overthinking can also weaken the immune system, making individuals more susceptible to illnesses. Sleep disturbances often accompany overthinking, further exacerbating the negative impact on mental health. Lack of quality sleep can lead to mood swings, irritability, and cognitive impairment, creating a vicious cycle that perpetuates the effects of overthinking on mental well-being.

In addition to the immediate emotional and psychological toll, chronic overthinking can also affect physical health in the long run. Individuals who engage in persistent overthinking may experience headaches, muscle tension, and digestive issues due to prolonged stress and anxiety. These physical symptoms not only contribute to discomfort but also serve as warning signs of deeper underlying issues related to mental health.

The long-term effects of overthinking can also strain interpersonal relationships, as individuals may become preoccupied with their thoughts and less present in their interactions. Constant worry and doubt can lead to misunderstandings, conflicts, and isolation from loved ones. This social impact further compounds the negative consequences of overthinking, creating a ripple effect beyond individual mental health.

Addressing the long-term effects of overthinking on mental health requires a holistic approach, focusing on both psychological well-being and physical health. Implementing stress-reducing techniques, such as mindfulness practices, exercise, and seeking professional help when needed, can be crucial in mitigating the detrimental outcomes of chronic overthinking. Creating healthy boundaries around thoughts and learning to challenge negative patterns can also contribute to long-term mental wellness.

By recognizing the lasting implications of overthinking on mental health, individuals can take proactive steps toward breaking free from this detrimental cycle. Building resilience, cultivating self-awareness, and nurturing positive coping mechanisms are essential in safeguarding mental well-being in the face of persistent overthinking. It is never too late to prioritize self-care and seek support in managing the long-term effects of overthinking, paving the way for a healthier mindset and improved quality of life.

Understanding the intricate relationship between overthinking and anxiety is crucial for anyone looking to improve their mental clarity and overall well-being. Through our exploration of this nexus, it's clear that overthinking fuels anxiety, creating a self-perpetuating cycle that can deeply impact mental health over time. Recognizing this pattern is the first step towards breaking free from its grip.

Persistent overthinking does not exist in isolation; it escalates anxiety by constantly triggering stress responses. This heightened stress can lead to mental exhaustion and a decreased quality of life. Acknowledging these effects as fleeting feelings and significant influencers on long-term health and happiness is essential.

To combat these challenges, adopting practical strategies is paramount. Simple yet effective techniques such as mindfulness, setting clear and achievable goals, and practicing regular self-reflection can significantly reduce the tendency to overthink. These methods help redirect focus from past and future worries to the present moment, fostering a sense of control and peace.

Encouragement to take active steps towards mental mastery is not just advice—it's necessary for those who find themselves caught in the whirlwind of their thoughts. Each small step taken is a move towards regaining control over your mental state, enhancing your ability to face life's challenges with resilience and calm.

Empower yourself by understanding that you can influence your thought patterns and reactions. The journey to improved mental health begins with awareness. It is sustained by the continuous application of effective strategies tailored to your personal needs.

Remember, overcoming overthinking and its associated anxieties involves commitment and practice. You are surviving and thriving by integrating these insights and techniques into your daily life. Each moment of mindfulness, each conscious decision to avoid redundant thoughts, significantly changes how you experience the world around you.

Moving forward, let this understanding empower you. You are capable of breaking the cycles of overthinking and anxiety, reclaiming not only your peace of mind but also enhancing your overall life experience.

Chapter 4: Rewiring Thoughts with CBT

"Realize deeply that the present moment

is all you ever have."

Eckhart Tolle

Transform Your Mind: How Cognitive-Behavioral Therapy Can Help You Stop Overthinking

Overthinking can feel like an endless battle within your mind, a cycle of thoughts that clouds clarity and consumes mental energy. However, cognitive-behaviral therapy (CBT) offers a powerful tool to break free from this exhausting loop. This chapter delves into how CBT can help you identify, challenge, and transform detrimental thought patterns into constructive responses, fostering mental clarity and peace.

CBT is grounded in the understanding that our thoughts, feelings, and behaviors are interconnected. By changing one component, we can influence the others. This idea is particularly liberating for those who often find themselves trapped in cycles of overthinking. The techniques taught in CBT empower individuals to disrupt these cycles at their origin—their thoughts—thereby mitigating the emotional and behavioral repercussions that follow.

Key Principles of Cognitive-Behavioral Therapy

The first step towards harnessing the power of CBT is understanding its core principles. These principles assert that not all thoughts are facts; many are simply perceptions heavily influenced by our biases and past experiences. Recognizing this discrepancy is crucial as it forms the basis for cognitive restructuring—an essential technique in CBT that we will explore further in this chapter.

Techniques for Cognitive Restructuring

Cognitive restructuring teaches you to identify irrational or harmful thoughts and challenge them systematically. This process helps recognize how unrealistic many of these thoughts are but also aids in developing healthier and more objective ways to view situations. It's about transforming "I always mess up" into "Everyone makes mistakes. I can learn from this," thereby reducing anxiety and enhancing problem-solving skills.

Applying CBT Methods to Break Overthinking

Practical application of CBT techniques will be covered extensively, providing actionable strategies to apply immediately. Whether you're dealing with stress at work, relationship issues, or personal insecurities, these methods can be tailored to address your specific needs and situations. The goal is to equip you with tools that combat overthinking when it occurs and prevent it from dominating your mental landscape in the future.

This chapter aims not just to inform but also to transform. You can actively alter your habitual thinking patterns by integrating CBT techniques into your daily life. It's about moving from passive absorption of relentless thoughts to actively reconfiguring your mental responses. You possess the innate ability to master your emotions and thoughts; this chapter will guide you on effectively using that power.

Remember, the journey toward mental clarity is progressive and requires patience and practice. However, with the consistent application of CBT strategies discussed here, achieving a calmer mind and clearer thought processes is not just a possibility but an achievable reality.

Let's embark on this transformative journey together—understanding the mechanics behind our thoughts, rewiring them through proven techniques, and reclaiming the mental peace that is inherently yours. Each step you take is a move towards a more empowered and serene mind.

Cognitive-behavioral therapy (CBT) is a powerful tool for combating overthinking by addressing the underlying thought patterns contributing to this cycle. Understanding the principles of CBT is crucial for individuals seeking to break free from the grip of excessive rumination. CBT operates on the premise that our thoughts influence our emotions and behaviors, and by altering these thoughts, we can transform our responses to various situations. This approach emphasizes the importance of identifying negative or distorted thinking patterns and replacing them with more balanced and realistic ones.

CBT Techniques: Cognitive restructuring, a core technique in CBT, involves challenging and changing irrational beliefs or cognitive distortions that fuel overthinking. By examining the evidence for and against these beliefs, individuals can gain a more objective perspective on their thoughts. This process helps develop healthier thinking habits that are less prone to catastrophic thinking or magnification of problems. Through guided exercises and self-reflection, individuals can learn to reframe their thoughts in a more positive and constructive light.

Reshaping Thoughts: The goal of CBT is not to eliminate all negative thoughts but rather to reframe them to promote mental well-being. By recognizing cognitive distortions such as black-and-white thinking, overgeneralization, or jumping to conclusions, individuals can challenge these patterns and replace them with more balanced interpretations. This process of cognitive restructuring empowers individuals to take control of their mental narratives and steer them towards healthier perspectives.

Breaking the Cycle: Overthinking often leads to a cycle of heightened anxiety and stress, perpetuating negative thought patterns. CBT equips individuals with the tools to interrupt this cycle by identifying triggers for overthinking and implementing coping strategies. Individuals can apply grounding techniques or mindfulness practices to return to the present moment by learning to recognize when they are slipping into overthinking mode.

Empowering Change: Understanding how thoughts impact emotions and behaviors is key to leveraging the power of CBT. By actively engaging in cognitive restructuring exercises, individuals can rewire their thought patterns over time, leading to lasting changes in their mental habits. Through consistent practice and application of CBT techniques, individuals can cultivate a more resilient mindset and be less susceptible to overthinking tendencies.

Techniques for Cognitive Restructuring

To counter irrational thoughts effectively, learning techniques for cognitive restructuring is essential. This process involves identifying negative or distorted thought patterns and replacing them with more balanced and realistic ones. Individuals can shift their mindset towards a healthier perspective by actively challenging and changing these harmful thoughts. One crucial technique in cognitive restructuring is recognizing cognitive distortions. These are inaccurate or biased ways of thinking that can contribute to overthinking and anxiety. By becoming aware of these distortions, individuals can challenge and reframe their thoughts more constructively.

Another valuable strategy in cognitive restructuring is thought-challenging. This technique involves questioning the validity of negative thoughts and examining evidence that supports or contradicts them. Individuals can break the cycle of automatic negative thinking and cultivate a more rational outlook by engaging in this process. Replacing irrational thoughts with more balanced alternatives is important, fostering a more positive and realistic view of oneself and the world.

Mindfulness techniques can also play a significant role in cognitive restructuring. By practicing mindfulness, individuals can observe their thoughts without judgment, allowing them to detach from negative thought patterns and create mental space for healthier perspectives. Mindfulness helps individuals become more aware of their thoughts and emotions, enabling them to respond to challenging situations with greater clarity and composure.

Behavioral experiments are another effective tool in cognitive restructuring. Individuals can gather evidence to support more adaptive thought patterns by testing new beliefs or behaviors in real-life situations. These experiments allow individuals to challenge their assumptions and beliefs, leading to a shift in perspective that promotes emotional well-being and reduces overthinking tendencies.

Self-Compassion Practices

Incorporating self-compassion practices into cognitive restructuring can enhance its effectiveness. Self-compassion involves treating oneself with kindness and understanding, especially during struggle or self-criticism. By cultivating self-compassion, individuals can develop a more forgiving attitude towards themselves, which can counteract the negative impact of overthinking.

Positive affirmations are another powerful tool in promoting self-compassion and reshaping thought patterns. By regularly affirming positive beliefs about oneself, individuals can counteract self-doubt and boost self-esteem. Affirmations help reinforce healthy thought patterns, fostering a sense of confidence and self-acceptance.

Journaling for Reflection

Journaling is an invaluable practice that complements cognitive restructuring by providing a structured outlet for reflection. Writing down thoughts and emotions allows individuals to gain insight into their mental processes and track patterns of overthinking. Through journaling, individuals can identify triggers for overthinking, challenge irrational beliefs, and celebrate victories in overcoming negative thinking patterns.

Journal prompts can be particularly helpful in guiding reflective writing sessions. These prompts encourage individuals to explore their thoughts, emotions, and experiences more deeply, fostering self-awareness and insight. By regularly journaling, individuals can monitor their progress in countering overthinking, track changes in their thought patterns, and reinforce positive habits developed through cognitive restructuring techniques.

Embracing Progress

As individuals engage with these techniques for cognitive restructuring, it is important to recognize that progress may not happen overnight. Change takes time, patience, and consistent effort. By embracing the journey of personal growth with compassion and perseverance, individuals can gradually rewire their thought patterns toward greater clarity and emotional well-being.

Taking Action

Implementing these strategies requires dedication and commitment but offers significant rewards in terms of mental clarity and reduced overthinking tendencies. By actively engaging with cognitive restructuring techniques, practicing self-compassion, incorporating mindfulness practices, conducting behavioral experiments, affirming positive beliefs through affirmations, journaling for reflection, and embracing progress with patience, individuals can empower themselves to break free from the cycle of overthinking and cultivate a mindset that promotes peace and resilience.

Cognitive Distortion Framework

The Cognitive Distortion Framework within the context of Cognitive-behavioral Therapy (CBT) aims to help individuals recognize and categorize distorted thinking patterns contributing to overthinking. By identifying common cognitive distortions such as 'All-or-Nothing Thinking,' 'Overgeneralization,' 'Mental Filtering,' 'Disqualifying the Positive,' 'Jumping to Conclusions,' 'Magnification and Minimization,' 'Emotional Reasoning,' 'Should Statements,' 'Labeling and Mislabeling,' and 'Personalization,' readers can begin to understand how these patterns impact their thought processes.

Each distortion presents a unique challenge, distorting reality in various ways. For example, 'All-or-Nothing Thinking' leads individuals to see situations in black or white terms without considering the gray areas. 'Jumping to Conclusions' involves making negative predictions without evidence. Recognizing these distortions is crucial in breaking the cycle of overthinking.

To challenge and reframe these distortions, individuals can utilize CBT techniques like questioning the evidence behind a thought, examining its usefulness, and exploring alternative perspectives. By transitioning from recognizing distorted thoughts to reconstructing them in a more balanced manner, individuals engage in cognitive restructuring, a core aspect of CBT. This process empowers individuals to shift from maladaptive to adaptive thinking patterns, fostering mental clarity and reducing overthinking tendencies.

Understanding the Cognitive Distortions

By diving into each cognitive distortion and understanding its impact on thought processes, individuals can gain insight into how these patterns fuel overthinking. Recognizing when these distortions arise is the first step towards challenging them effectively.

Challenging and Reframing Distortions

Individuals can start unraveling their overthinking tendencies by questioning distorted thoughts' validity. By examining the usefulness of these thoughts and considering alternative viewpoints, individuals can gradually reframe their thinking in a more constructive light.

Transition to Adaptive Thinking

The journey from recognizing cognitive distortions to actively restructuring thoughts represents a fundamental shift toward adaptive thinking. By implementing CBT techniques consistently, individuals can break free from the cycle of overthinking and cultivate a more balanced mindset.

Incorporating this Cognitive Distortion Framework into daily practice equips individuals with valuable tools to combat overthinking effectively. By challenging distorted thoughts and reshaping them through cognitive restructuring, individuals pave the way for mental clarity and emotional well-being.

Cognitive-behavioral therapy (CBT) emerges as a powerful ally in our quest to combat overthinking, offering structured methods to rewire our thought processes toward more rational and positive outcomes. This chapter has equipped you with the understanding and practical steps necessary to apply CBT effectively in your daily life, fostering mental clarity and emotional resilience.

Step-by-Step Guide: "Clear Mind Blueprint"

Objective: To systematically apply CBT techniques to reduce overthinking and enhance mental well-being.

1. Understand the Principles of CBT Familiarize yourself with CBT's focus on altering detrimental thought patterns and behaviors. Recognize its potential to curb overthinking and sharpen your mental clarity.
2. Identify Negative Thought Patterns Begin by pinpointing the recurring negative thoughts that fuel your tendency to overthink. Acknowledge these patterns as the first step towards change.
3. Challenge Irrational Thoughts: With your negative

thoughts identified, rigorously question their validity. Employ questions like, "Is this thought factual or based on assumptions?" This helps to dismantle the power of irrational beliefs.

4. Replace Negative Thoughts
   Substitute irrational or negative thoughts with more balanced, positive ones. Transform thoughts like "I always fail" into "Every experience is a learning opportunity."

5. Practice Cognitive Restructuring Techniques
   Integrate techniques that allow you to reframe negative thoughts constructively into your daily routine, gradually reshaping your mental landscape.

6. Monitor and Challenge Overthinking: Stay vigilant about your thought patterns. When overthinking, consciously redirect your focus towards more constructive thoughts.

7. Practice Self-Compassion: Approach this process with kindness and patience. Change is a journey; self-recognition of your efforts is crucial in sustaining progress.
   Timeframe: Implement these steps over weeks, allowing each phase to naturally integrate into your daily habits. Regular practice will lead to noticeable improvements in your thought processes and overall mental health.

By following this "Clear Mind Blueprint," you are not just learning to manage overthinking; you are taking active steps towards a more balanced and fulfilling mental state. Each step is designed to build upon the last, gradually enhancing your ability to control and direct your thoughts effectively.

Remember, the path to mastering your mind is both challenging and rewarding. Each small victory in this journey contributes to a greater sense of control and peace in your life. Embrace these techniques, practice diligently, and watch as you transform your mental landscape into one that supports and nurtures your well-being.

Chapter 5: The Power of Presence

"The unexamined life is not worth living."

Socrates

Discover the Freedom of Now: Embrace Mindfulness to Shatter Mental Clutter

Mindfulness emerges as a profound ally in a world where our thoughts often race ahead without permission. This practice isn't just about quieting the mind but transforming our relationship with our thoughts. For those frequently caught in the whirlwind of overthinking, mindfulness offers a grounding technique to manage this tendency and enhance overall mental clarity. The essence of mindfulness is simple yet powerful: it teaches us to reside fully in the present moment, acknowledging thoughts without becoming entangled in them.

Understanding Mindfulness

Mindfulness is the foundational step towards gaining control over persistent overthinking. It involves an attentive awareness of the present moment, free from distraction and judgment. Learning to anchor ourselves in the now allows us to observe our thoughts and feelings without criticism. This process doesn't stop thoughts from coming but changes our reaction to them. Here lies the crux of mindfulness: it empowers us to recognize our mental patterns without being dominated by them, thereby reducing stress and anxiety.

Engaging with Practical Exercises

The journey into mindfulness isn't merely theoretical but deeply practical. Engaging in focused breathing exercises and meditation are actionable strategies that bring about significant shifts in our mental state. These practices offer immediate relief from the clutches of rumination, providing a space to reset and refocus. In this chapter, we will explore specific exercises that you can incorporate into your daily routine, ensuring that these techniques are not only accessible but also adaptable to your personal needs.

Alleviating Intrusive Thoughts

One of the greatest benefits of staying present through mindfulness is alleviating intrusive thoughts. These unwelcome visitors often disrupt our peace and can spiral into excessive worrying or anxiety. Through mindfulness, we learn to address these thoughts by acknowledging their presence and letting them pass without engaging further. This approach is profoundly liberating as it cuts through the noise and clutter, fostering a sense of calm and control.

Mindfulness is a practice and a way of living that enhances our mental resilience and clarity. By dedicating time to understanding and engaging with mindfulness techniques, you are taking proactive steps towards not just managing to overthink but thriving despite it. The practices outlined here are designed to be integrated seamlessly into your life, allowing you to cultivate presence and peace amidst life's chaos.

Remember, mastering your mind is not about achieving a perfect state devoid of thought but about enhancing your ability to harmonize with your thoughts. As you embark on this journey through mindfulness, you embrace a powerful tool that supports ongoing mental health and clarity, proving essential in breaking free from the binds of overthinking.

Take control: start small with mindful moments each day, and observe as your relationship with your thoughts—and consequently your life—transforms profoundly.

Mindfulness serves as a powerful tool to combat the incessant chatter of overthinking. By focusing on the present moment without judgment, individuals can cultivate awareness to observe their thoughts without becoming entangled. This practice creates a mental space where one can acknowledge thoughts as they arise and then let them go rather than allowing them to spiral out of control.

Engaging in mindfulness practices like meditation and focused breathing can help individuals develop the ability to stay present and centered. Through regular practice, individuals can train their minds to redirect attention to the current moment whenever it wanders into a cycle of overthinking. By honing this skill, individuals can break free from the grip of intrusive thoughts and cultivate a greater sense of mental clarity and peace.

Mindfulness is not about eliminating thoughts altogether but changing our relationship with them. Instead of getting caught up in the stories our minds create, mindfulness encourages us to observe our thoughts from a place of detachment. This shift in perspective allows us to see thoughts for what they are—transient mental events that do not define us.

One key aspect of mindfulness is the emphasis on non-judgmental awareness. Rather than labeling thoughts as good or bad, right or wrong, mindfulness encourages us to observe them without attaching value judgments. By adopting this approach, individuals can reduce the emotional charge associated with their thoughts, leading to a more balanced and grounded state of mind.

Practicing mindfulness requires consistency and dedication, but the benefits are worth the effort. Over time, individuals may notice a significant reduction in overthinking, increased emotional resilience, and improved overall well-being. By integrating mindfulness into daily life, individuals can learn to navigate their inner landscape with greater ease and grace, freeing themselves from the shackles of overthinking.

Engaging in Focused Breathing and Meditation

Focused Breathing: One of the simplest yet most powerful mindfulness practices is focused breathing. It involves directing your attention to your breath, using it as an anchor to the present moment. Start by finding a quiet and comfortable place to sit or lie down. Close your eyes and take a deep breath through your nose, feeling your lungs expand. Then, exhale slowly through your mouth, releasing any tension you may be holding. Repeat this process several times, focusing solely on the sensation of breathing in and out. Notice how the air feels as it enters and leaves your body without judgment or analysis. This exercise can be done for a few minutes or extended longer, depending on your comfort level.

Meditation: Meditation is a practice that cultivates mindfulness by training the mind to focus and redirect thoughts. Begin by finding a peaceful environment to sit comfortably with your back straight. Close your eyes and bring your attention to the present moment. You can focus on your breath, a specific mantra, or simply observe your thoughts without getting caught up. As distractions arise, gently acknowledge them and then return your focus to your chosen point of attention. Meditation is not about emptying the mind but observing thoughts without attachment. Over time, this practice can help you become more aware of your thought patterns and emotions, allowing you to respond consciously rather than react impulsively.

Combining Techniques: Combining focused breathing with meditation can enhance the benefits of both practices. Start with a few minutes of focused breathing to center yourself in the present moment. Then, transition into a meditation session, using the stability gained from focused breathing to deepen your awareness. By incorporating these techniques into your daily routine, you can build resilience against overthinking and cultivate a sense of calm amidst life's challenges.

Consistency is Key: Like any skill, mindfulness requires consistent practice to yield significant results. Set aside dedicated time each day for these exercises, even if it's just for a few minutes initially. Over time, you'll notice improvements in staying present and letting go of intrusive thoughts. Remember that progress may not always be linear, and having days where concentration feels challenging is okay. Be gentle with yourself and approach each session with an open mind and heart.

Creating Your Routine: Establishing a routine incorporating focused breathing and meditation can help make these practices a natural part of your day. Consider integrating them into your morning or evening rituals, aligning them with times you're less likely to be interrupted. Experiment with different durations and techniques to find what works best for you. Consistency is more important than intensity; even short sessions done regularly can have profound effects on reducing overthinking and increasing mental clarity.

By regularly engaging in practical exercises like focused breathing and meditation, you empower yourself to take control of your thoughts and emotions. These simple yet profound practices offer a pathway to greater self-awareness and inner peace. Embrace the power of presence through mindfulness techniques, allowing yourself to experience life fully in each moment without being consumed by overthinking or anxiety.

Staying present and learning to alleviate the grip of intrusive thoughts is a skill that can be developed with practice and patience. Mindfulness techniques, such as meditation and focused breathing, play a crucial role in helping individuals break free from the cycle of overthinking. By cultivating an awareness of the present moment without judgment, individuals can begin to acknowledge intrusive thoughts and let them go rather than become entangled in them.

One key aspect of staying present is recognizing that intrusive thoughts are normal and do not define who we are. Observing these thoughts without attachment or reaction can gradually diminish their power over our mental state. Mindfulness encourages us to approach these thoughts with curiosity and openness, allowing us to explore their origins without getting caught up in their emotional grip.

Practical exercises like focused breathing and meditation provide tangible tools for staying present. Through these practices, individuals can anchor themselves in the current moment, fostering a sense of calm and clarity to help manage overwhelming thoughts. By incorporating these exercises into daily routines, individuals can cultivate a habit of mindfulness that supports their mental well-being.

Learning to stay present also involves developing a compassionate attitude towards oneself. Instead of harshly judging intrusive thoughts or becoming frustrated with our mind's tendency to wander, we must offer ourselves kindness and understanding. By practicing self-compassion, we create a supportive inner environment that allows us to easily navigate challenging thoughts.

Alleviating the grip of intrusive thoughts requires consistent effort and dedication. Returning to the present moment whenever we notice our minds drifting towards overthinking reinforces our ability to stay grounded and focused. Through regular practice, individuals can strengthen their mindfulness skills, gradually reducing the frequency and intensity of intrusive thoughts.

Remember, staying present is a skill that improves with time and practice. Each moment presents an opportunity to choose awareness over automatic thinking patterns, empowering us to break free from the cycle of overthinking. By cultivating mindfulness, individuals can experience greater mental clarity, reduced stress, and enhanced well-being in their daily lives.

As we've explored the transformative potential of mindfulness, it's clear that embracing this practice can significantly reduce the impact of overthinking and intrusive thoughts. Mindfulness fosters mental clarity and strengthens our emotional resilience by centering on the present. This chapter has provided a foundation for developing a robust mindfulness routine that can be a powerful tool in navigating the challenges of overthinking.

The Process: "Mindful Mastery Steps"

This process integrates mindfulness into your daily life, enabling you to cultivate a sense of calm and focus. Following these steps, you'll learn to manage your thoughts effectively and enhance your overall well-being.

Step 1: Learn the Basics of Mindfulness

Begin by grasping the essence of mindfulness—focusing on the present moment with a nonjudgmental mindset. This understanding is crucial as it underpins all further practices in mindfulness and its benefits in curbing overthinking.

Step 2: Begin with Focused Breathing

Engage in simple breathing exercises. Find a serene spot, take slow, deep breaths, and let your mind settle. This practice lays the groundwork for deeper mindfulness exercises and helps anchor your focus.

Step 3: Incorporate Meditation into Your Routine

Establish a regular meditation schedule. Even a few minutes daily can profoundly impact your ability to stay present and diminish the noise of intrusive thoughts.

Step 4: Practice Non-Judgmental Observation

While meditating, observe your thoughts passively. Acknowledge them without engagement and gently redirect your focus to your breath or a chosen object of meditation whenever distractions arise.

Step 5: Cultivate Daily Mindfulness

Expand the practice beyond structured exercises. Integrate mindfulness into everyday activities like eating or walking. This continuous practice enhances your ability to remain present throughout the day.

Step 6: Utilize Mindfulness Apps or Resources

Leverage technology by using apps or online resources that guide you through various mindfulness exercises. These tools provide structured support to help maintain your practice.

Step 7: Be Patient and Persistent

Recognize that developing mindfulness is a journey. Consistent practice is key to gaining full benefits, so maintain your dedication and be patient with your progress.

Through these steps, you will learn to manage to overthink and discover how to live more fully in the moment. Each step builds upon the last, reinforcing the skills needed to sustain mindfulness and ensuring you have the tools to combat intrusive thoughts effectively.

Integrating these practices into your life takes a significant step toward mental clarity and emotional stability. Remember, each mindful moment is a step toward a calmer, more centered self. Keep pushing forward, using these techniques as your guide, and watch as overthinking loses its hold over your life.

Chapter 6: Structured Thinking for Unstructured Minds

"You are the sky. Everything else –

it's just the weather."

Pema Chödrön

Harness the Power of Structured Thinking

It's all too common to find ourselves caught in the whirlpool of overthinking, where every problem seems insurmountable, and solutions seem just out of reach. This often leads to a cycle of anxiety and unproductive worrying. However, there is a powerful strategy that can not only break this cycle but also transform it into a constructive force. By adopting structured problem-solving techniques, you can channel your mental energy into more productive avenues, preventing aimless worrying and enhancing your overall mental clarity.

Embrace the Strategy of Deliberate Thinking

One might wonder how simply changing the way we approach problems can have such a profound impact on our mental state. The answer lies in the deliberate structuring of thought processes. When you designate specific times to think about your problems, you create a controlled environment for your mind to engage with these issues. This prevents the mind from returning to these worries outside the allotted times, significantly reducing habitual overthinking.

Channel Your Overthinking

Overthinking doesn't have to be a detriment; it can be redirected towards productive outcomes. Developing skills to harness this tendency can turn what is often seen as a weakness into one of your greatest strengths. By learning to focus your thoughts and keep them within structured bounds, you solve problems more effectively and free up mental space for other important activities and thoughts.

Set Boundaries for Your Thoughts

The practice of setting specific times for deliberation is crucial in preventing the overflow of uncontrolled anxiety and worry into every corner of your life. It's about creating mental compartments—specific times and spaces where problem-solving happens. Outside these times, the mind can rest or engage in other healthier thinking patterns. This improves mental health and boosts productivity by keeping you focused on solutions during designated periods.

Structured thinking is more than just a method; it's a skill that enhances life quality by fostering mental discipline and clarity. This chapter will delve deeper into practical ways to implement these strategies effectively, ensuring readers can apply them seamlessly into their daily routines.

Remember, mastering your mind is not about suppressing thoughts but organizing them so that they serve you rather than control you. Engaging with structured problem-solving is akin to training your mind to operate more efficiently and less chaotically.

By the end of this chapter, you will be equipped with tools not just to cope with overthinking but to actively redirect it towards achieving personal goals and maintaining peace of mind. Embracing these practices means taking significant steps towards unlocking mental clarity and leading a calmer, more focused life.

Structured problem-solving techniques are powerful tools to help break the cycle of aimless worrying and overthinking. By implementing structured approaches to tackle problems, individuals can navigate their thoughts more effectively and arrive at solutions with clarity. Setting aside dedicated time to engage in structured problem-solving can prevent the mind from wandering into unproductive avenues of rumination. This deliberate structuring of thought creates a framework for organizing ideas and considerations, leading to more efficient decision-making processes.

One effective technique for structured problem-solving is breaking down complex issues into smaller, more manageable components. Individuals can approach a problem systematically and methodically by dissecting it into its constituent parts. This approach helps avoid being overwhelmed and promotes a sense of control over the situation. Creating a step-by-step plan or roadmap toward a solution can provide a clear path forward, reducing the tendency to get lost in endless loops of worry.

Another valuable strategy is setting specific goals and objectives when approaching a problem. Defining what needs improvement helps focus thoughts and actions toward meaningful outcomes. Individuals can track their progress and stay motivated throughout the problem-solving process by establishing measurable targets. A clear endpoint can prevent the mind from spiraling into uncertainty and doubt.

Moreover, employing tools such as mind mapping or brainstorming can aid in generating creative solutions and exploring different perspectives. These techniques encourage divergent thinking, allowing for the exploration of various possibilities before converging on the most suitable course of action. Collaborative problem-solving activities can also provide fresh insights and new approaches to challenging situations.

Structured Problem-solving Techniques

Developing the skills to channel this mental energy into productive outcomes is key to conquering overthinking. Rather than letting thoughts swirl endlessly without purpose, directing them toward constructive avenues is vital. By honing your ability to steer overthinking towards actionable solutions, you can transform a potential source of stress into a powerful tool for problem-solving.

One effective strategy is to practice mindfulness. By staying present in the moment and focusing on the task, you can prevent your mind from wandering down paths of overanalysis. Mindfulness helps bring awareness to your thoughts and emotions, allowing you to observe them without getting entangled. This practice empowers you to recognize when overthinking patterns emerge and allows you to redirect your focus.

Another valuable skill is learning to differentiate between productive thinking and rumination. While productive thinking involves actively seeking solutions and making decisions, rumination tends to be circular and unproductive, leading to increased anxiety. By consciously steering your thoughts towards problem-solving rather than dwelling on problems, you can break free from the cycle of overthinking and move toward resolution.

Setting boundaries for your thoughts is essential. Establish specific times during the day dedicated to deliberate problem-solving or planning. Confining your worries to these designated periods prevents them from infiltrating every moment of your day. This structured approach enhances productivity by allocating time for focused thinking. It helps reduce overall stress levels by containing overthinking tendencies.

Practice reframing negative thoughts into positive action steps. Instead of letting worries consume you, transform them into actionable goals or tasks. By shifting your perspective from dwelling on problems to seeking solutions, you harness the energy of overthinking toward progress. This shift in mindset empowers you to take control of your thoughts and turn them into catalysts for growth.

Remember that developing skills to channel overthinking into productive outcomes is a process that requires practice and patience. Be gentle with yourself as you navigate this journey, understanding that change takes time and effort. Embrace each small step forward as a victory in breaking free from the chains of endless rumination. Dedication and perseverance can transform overthinking from a hindrance into a valuable asset in navigating life's challenges.

Setting specific times for deliberation can be a powerful tool in breaking the cycle of habitual worrying. By allocating dedicated moments to address concerns and brainstorm solutions, individuals can prevent their minds from wandering aimlessly into overthinking. Establishing structured problem-solving periods helps redefine the tendency to fret constantly, offering a more focused approach to dealing with challenges. This deliberate allocation of time for reflection and analysis serves as a boundary that contains worries within manageable limits.

By setting aside designated slots for contemplation, individuals can train their minds to save deep thought for appropriate moments rather than allowing worries to infiltrate every aspect of their day. This practice helps compartmentalize concerns, create mental space for other activities, and reduce the overwhelming burden of perpetual overthinking. Having scheduled times for deliberation instills a sense of control over thoughts and emotions, empowering individuals to approach problems with clarity and purpose.

Consistency is key when it comes to establishing specific times for contemplation. Regularity in these sessions cultivates a disciplined mindset and reinforces the habit of constructive problem-solving over fretful rumination. By adhering to a set schedule, individuals condition their minds to engage productively with challenges at designated intervals, thus minimizing the intrusive nature of habitual worrying throughout the day.

Creating a routine around deliberation periods can serve as an anchor amidst the turbulent waters of overthinking. These structured moments act as anchors that ground individuals in proactive problem-solving, steering them away from the whirlpool of endless worries. By adhering to predetermined times for reflection, individuals establish a sense of stability and control, enabling them to navigate challenges with resilience and composure.

Setting specific times for deliberation is an act of self-care and empowerment. It signifies a commitment to mental well-being and personal growth, highlighting individuals' proactive management of their thoughts and emotions. By prioritizing structured thinking, individuals pave the way for greater clarity and peace of mind, fostering a healthier relationship with their inner dialogue and external challenges.

Engaging in structured problem-solving is not just a method; it's a transformative practice that reorients our mental processes, steering us away from the cyclical trap of overthinking and guiding us toward clarity and actionable solutions. By implementing the strategies discussed in this chapter, you harness the power of structured thinking, turning what might once have been a source of stress into a wellspring of productivity.

Pathway to Clarity: A Structured Problem-Solving Process

Step 1: Recognize the Need for Structured Thinking

Understanding the benefits of structured thinking is crucial. It helps manage and significantly reduce overthinking, often due to a disorganized problem-solving approach.

Step 2: Define the Problem

Start by clearly identifying the issue at hand. Break it down into manageable parts to better understand the underlying factors.

Step 3: Generate Multiple Solutions

Encourage a brainstorming session where quantity trumps quality. The goal here is to explore as many avenues as possible without judgment.

Step 4: Evaluate and Prioritize Solutions

Assess each solution based on feasibility and potential benefits. Prioritize them so that you can focus your efforts on the most promising solutions.

Step 5: Create an Action Plan

Choose the best solution and develop a detailed plan of action. Include specific steps and deadlines to ensure accountability.

Step 6: Take Action

Implement your plan diligently. Focus on the outlined steps, avoiding falling back into overthinking.

Step 7: Evaluate and Adjust

Regularly assess your progress and be prepared to make adjustments. Flexibility here is key to overcoming unforeseen challenges.

Step 8: Reflect and Learn

After action, take time to reflect on the outcomes. Identify what worked and what didn't, gathering insights to improve future problem-solving efforts.

Following these steps empowers you to transform unstructured, anxiety-driven thought patterns into organized, constructive mental processes. Each step is designed to tackle the immediate problem and build your skills in handling future challenges more efficiently.

Embrace this process as a part of your daily life and watch as your mental clarity improves, your anxiety wanes, and your productivity soars. Remember, the goal is not to eliminate all worrying but to manage it so effectively that it no longer controls you but serves you.

Chapter 7: Journaling the Jumbled Thoughts

"Mindfulness means being awake. It means

knowing what you are doing."

Jon Kabat-Zinn

Harness the Power of Pen and Paper to Soothe Your Mind

Journaling is often viewed as a simple diary entry, a recap of the day's events, or a list of what we hope tomorrow will bring. However, when harnessed correctly, journaling is a powerful therapeutic tool that can significantly aid in managing overthinking and enhancing mental clarity. This chapter delves into how putting pen to paper can transform jumbled thoughts into structured insights, thereby reducing anxiety and promoting emotional well-being.

Many of us grapple with the relentless churn of thoughts that clutter our minds daily. These thoughts can range from minor worries about daily chores to profound concerns about life's direction. Writing them down can act as a release valve, providing a physical space for these thoughts and allowing you to see them outside the confines of your mind. By externalizing them, you can evaluate and manage them more effectively.

Understanding Journaling as Therapy

The benefits of journaling are supported by numerous psychological studies. It has been shown to improve mood, reduce stress, and even enhance immune function. But its most compelling benefit for those who overthink is its ability to clarify thoughts and emotions. Writing down what you feel or think helps organize the chaos in your head into coherent threads that are easier to understand and address.

Techniques That Offer Relief

In exploring various journaling techniques, we focus on those designed to help externalize and process overthinking. Techniques such as stream-of-consciousness writing or bullet journaling can particularly be beneficial. These methods record thoughts as they occur and play a crucial role in dissecting and understanding them. Each technique offers a unique way to engage with your thoughts and can be tailored to personal preferences and needs.

Exploring Styles for Every Mind

Moreover, this chapter will guide you through different journaling styles—each suited for various types of thinkers and scenarios. Whether it's daily reflective journaling, gratitude journaling, or problem-solving journaling, understanding how to use each style can significantly affect managing anxiety and overthinking. The key is to find which style resonates with you most and makes the process enjoyable rather than a chore.

Journaling is about managing negative thoughts and fostering an environment where positive thoughts have room to grow. It encourages a habit of mindfulness where one becomes keenly aware of one's mental habits—what triggers stress or anxiety and what alleviates it. This awareness is the first step towards lasting mental clarity.

Actionable advice will be provided throughout this exploration—simple steps to integrate into your daily routine without feeling overwhelmed by drastic changes. The aim is to inform and empower you to take control of your mental landscape.

Engaging actively with these strategies will lessen the burden of overthinking and enhance your overall emotional resilience. Journaling offers a path toward tranquility amidst the tumults of life—a tool at once simple yet profoundly effective in achieving mental clarity and peace.

Journaling can be a powerful tool for gaining mental clarity and managing overthinking. By putting our thoughts on paper, we externalize them, making them easier to process and understand. Writing down our concerns can help us see them from a different perspective and reduce the intensity of our overthinking. Through journaling, we can navigate the maze of our thoughts and emotions with more clarity and insight.

We create a tangible record of our inner struggles by writing down our jumbled thoughts. This process lets us observe our thinking patterns objectively, helping us identify recurring themes or triggers contributing to our overthinking. Journaling provides a safe space for self-reflection and introspection, fostering greater self-awareness and understanding of our mental processes.

Moreover, journaling can serve as a form of emotional release. By expressing our worries, fears, and anxieties on paper, we unload the burden they place on our minds. Releasing pent-up emotions can be incredibly cathartic and freeing, offering relief and emotional lightness.

In addition to aiding in emotional processing, journaling can help us organize our thoughts more effectively. When we transfer our chaotic internal dialogue onto paper, we create a structured framework that can lead to insights and solutions. This organized approach can assist in breaking down complex issues into manageable parts, making it easier to address them with clarity and purpose.

The Power of Journaling in Managing Overthinking

Journaling is a powerful tool that can assist in externalizing and processing overthinking. By putting pen to paper, you can effectively transfer the jumbled thoughts from your mind onto a physical medium, allowing for better clarity and understanding. This journaling helps organize chaotic thoughts, making them more manageable and less overwhelming.

One effective technique in journaling is the practice of stream-of-consciousness writing. This involves writing down your thoughts as they come to you without filtering or censoring them. It can be a liberating experience, providing insight into the inner workings of your mind. By allowing your thoughts to flow freely onto the page, you may discover patterns or recurring themes contributing to your overthinking tendencies.

Another helpful journaling technique is creating lists or bullet points. This method can help structure your thoughts in a more organized manner, making it easier to identify specific areas of concern. Listing out your worries or anxieties can provide a clear visual representation of what is troubling you, enabling you to address each issue individually.

Visual journaling is another creative approach to processing overthinking. Using images, colors, or symbols alongside written entries can add another dimension to your journaling practice. Visual elements can evoke emotions and memories that words alone may not capture, offering a holistic way to explore and express your thoughts.

Reflective journaling prompts can guide your writing toward deeper introspection. Asking yourself targeted questions such as "What triggered this thought?" or "How do I feel about this situation?" can prompt self-reflection and lead to valuable insights. These prompts encourage you to delve beneath the surface of your thoughts, uncovering underlying emotions and beliefs.

Gratitude journaling is an uplifting practice that can counterbalance negative overthinking tendencies. By focusing on things you are grateful for daily, you shift your perspective towards positivity and abundance. Acknowledging the good in your life through journaling can cultivate a sense of appreciation and contentment, reducing the space for incessant worrying.

Incorporating these diverse journaling techniques into your routine can provide a multifaceted approach to managing overthinking. Experiment with different methods to find what resonates most with you and adapt your journaling practice accordingly. Remember that journaling is a personal journey of self-discovery and growth; there is no right or wrong way to journal, only what works best for you in navigating the labyrinth of overthinking.

Journaling can take various forms, each offering unique benefits for managing and reducing anxiety. Bullet Journaling is a popular method that combines creativity with organization. By designing your journal layout, you can personalize it to suit your needs and preferences, making the process enjoyable and engaging. Gratitude Journaling involves focusing on the positive aspects of life, which can shift your mindset from negative to positive, reducing anxiety. By regularly noting down things you are grateful for, you train your brain to seek the good in every situation.

Stream-of-Consciousness Journaling is a technique where you write continuously without worrying about grammar or structure. This form of journaling allows you to release pent-up emotions and thoughts without judgment, helping to clear your mind of clutter and reduce overthinking. Prompts Journaling involves using specific questions or topics to guide your writing. This method can help you delve deeper into your thoughts and emotions, providing insights into the root causes of your anxiety.

Art Journaling combines writing with visual expression through drawing, painting, or collage. This creative approach allows for a non-verbal exploration of emotions, providing a holistic way to process anxiety and overthinking. Travel Journaling can transport you to different places mentally, offering a break from everyday stressors. By documenting your thoughts and experiences during travels or even imaginary journeys, you can distract yourself from overthinking and find moments of peace.

Dream Journaling involves recording your dreams upon waking up. Dreams can be rich sources of subconscious thoughts and emotions that may contribute to anxiety. By analyzing your dreams through journaling, you may uncover hidden fears or concerns that could fuel overthinking. Bullet Points Journaling is a concise method that involves jotting down quick notes or lists instead of paragraphs. This style effectively captures fleeting thoughts and organizes information clearly and in a structured way.

Experiment with different journaling styles to find what resonates most with you. Combining multiple techniques or switching between them based on mood can keep the practice fresh and engaging. Remember that journaling is a personal journey; there is no right or wrong way. The key is to find a style that helps you manage anxiety and reduce overthinking effectively while promoting self-reflection and emotional well-being.

Journaling is more than just a method to capture daily events; it is a powerful tool for mental clarity and emotional regulation. By writing down your thoughts, you can transform your approach to overthinking and anxiety. This process helps externalize feelings and view them from a new, less intimidating perspective.

The Power of Processing Thoughts Through Writing

Journaling encourages you to slow down and engage with your thoughts systematically. It allows you to identify patterns in your thinking that may contribute to your stress. Once these patterns are visible, they become manageable. Journaling doesn't just help clarify thoughts; it offers a chance to rethink and reframe them, providing practical solutions to seemingly overwhelming problems.

Embracing Various Journaling Styles

Exploring different styles of journaling can significantly enhance its effectiveness. Whether bullet journaling, stream of consciousness, or structured writing prompts, each method offers unique benefits. These techniques ensure that journaling remains a fresh and flexible tool, adaptable to your changing needs and circumstances. This adaptability is crucial in maintaining a consistent journaling practice supporting mental health.

Actionable Steps Forward

To integrate journaling into your life effectively, start with small, consistent entries. Even a few minutes each day can make a significant difference. Keep your journal easily accessible, and make it a habit to write in it during a particular time of the day that suits you best. Remember, the goal is not perfection but progress. Over time, this simple practice can lead to profound insights and emotional balance.

Journaling stands out as a self-empowered approach to managing mental clutter and anxiety. It equips you with the skills to actively observe and modify your thoughts, fostering a calmer, more reflective mind. As you move forward, let journaling be your ally in the journey towards greater mental clarity and reduced anxiety. Embrace this tool, and watch as it transforms your thoughts and overall well-being.

Chapter 8: Moving Beyond the Mind

What lies behind us and what lies before us

are tiny matters compared to

what lies within us."

Ralph Waldo Emerson

Unravel the Chains: How Breaking Ruminative Thoughts Leads to Mental Liberation

Ruminative thought patterns are often the hidden culprits behind a foggy mind and persistent anxiety. These repetitive, negative thought cycles can trap us in a state of mental paralysis, where clarity and peace seem out of reach. This chapter delves into understanding these patterns, identifying their triggers, and effectively breaking free from their grip to achieve mental clarity.

The journey to mental liberation begins with recognizing how ruminative thinking fuels overthinking. By continuously dwelling on the same distressing thoughts, individuals inadvertently amplify their anxiety and obstruct their capacity for clear thinking. This realization is pivotal as it sets the stage for transformative change—moving from passive rumination to active management of one's mental landscape.

Key Insights on the Pathway to Clarity

Firstly, we explore the profound impact of physical activity on mental health. Engaging in regular physical exercise is not merely about enhancing physical well-being but also about fortifying mental health. Physical activity acts as a powerful countermeasure against stress and anxiety, offering a natural escape from the relentless cycle of ruminative thoughts.

Next, we uncover various exercises designed to combat stress and overthinking. These exercises are not one-size-fits-all; they are tailored to fit different lifestyles and preferences, ensuring everyone can find a method that resonates with them. These activities, from mindfulness practices to structured physical workouts, provide practical tools to disrupt overthinking and foster a calm mind.

Incorporating regular physical activity into one's routine is more than just a distraction—it is a strategic approach to diverting mental energy away from destructive patterns and towards constructive engagement. This shift is crucial in maintaining long-term mental clarity and resilience.

Strategies for Sustainable Change

Developing a routine that integrates these exercises seamlessly into daily life is essential to make these changes lasting. Consistency is key in transforming temporary relief into enduring tranquility. Moreover, understanding the underlying triggers of ruminative thinking enables individuals to anticipate and mitigate potential setbacks, maintaining control over their thought processes.

The ultimate goal is to manage symptoms and initiate a profound internal shift that redefines one's relationship with one's thoughts. By mastering ruminative patterns, individuals empower themselves to lead lives of greater peace, clarity, and purpose.

This chapter guides this transformative journey, offering compassionate insights and practical strategies tailored to help you reclaim your mental space. Embrace these tools with an open heart and a committed mind, and watch as you move beyond mere coping into thriving—a state where clarity isn't just possible; it's inevitable.

Physical activity plays a crucial role in influencing mental health.

Engaging in regular exercise has been shown to have numerous benefits for the mind, including reducing symptoms of anxiety and depression. When we move our bodies, we release endorphins, often called the "feel-good" hormones, which can help elevate mood and combat feelings of stress and overthinking. Additionally, physical activity promotes better sleep patterns, which is essential for overall mental well-being.

Exercise is beneficial for the body; it directly impacts our mental state. Incorporating physical activity into our daily routines can improve our cognitive function, boost our self-esteem, and enhance our overall quality of life. The connection between physical movement and mental health is profound and should not be underestimated. Even small amounts of exercise can significantly affect how we think and feel.

Moreover, physical activity provides a healthy outlet for releasing pent-up emotions and tension. Instead of ruminating on negative thoughts or getting caught up in a cycle of overthinking, exercise allows us to channel that energy into something productive and positive. Movement becomes a form of therapy, helping us clear our minds and gain perspective on our thoughts.

The mind-body connection is undeniable; what we do with our bodies directly impacts our mental state. By prioritizing physical activity, we are caring for our physical health and nurturing our emotional well-being. Exercise is a powerful tool that can help break the cycle of overthinking by redirecting our focus away from intrusive thoughts toward the present moment.

Exercises to Combat Stress and Overthinking

Physical exercise is a powerful tool in combating stress and overthinking. Engaging in regular physical activity can significantly impact mental health, providing a much-needed break from the incessant rumination that often plagues those prone to overthinking. Exercise has been shown to release endorphins, the body's natural feel-good chemicals, which can help reduce feelings of anxiety and depression. By incorporating various exercises into your routine, you can work towards breaking free from the cycle of negative thoughts and overwhelming worries.

Cardiovascular exercises like running, cycling, or swimming boost mood and reduce stress levels. These activities increase blood flow to the brain, promoting the release of neurotransmitters like serotonin and dopamine, which are essential for regulating emotions. Cardiovascular exercises can help improve sleep quality, another crucial factor in managing stress and anxiety. By committing to regular cardio workouts, you can experience enhanced mental clarity and a more positive outlook.

Strength training is another valuable exercise modality for combating overthinking. Not only does it improve physical health by building muscle strength and endurance, but it also has significant mental health benefits. Strength training releases endorphins like cardiovascular exercise, offering a natural mood boost and reducing anxiety symptoms. Moreover, the sense of accomplishment that comes with progressing in strength training can boost self-esteem and confidence, counteracting the negative self-talk often associated with overthinking.

Mind-body exercises, such as yoga and Pilates, offer a unique blend of physical movement and mindfulness practices that particularly benefit those struggling with overthinking. These exercises focus on breath control, meditation, and gentle movements that promote relaxation and stress relief. By incorporating mind-body exercises into your routine, you can cultivate a sense of presence and mindfulness that helps counteract the tendency to get lost in unproductive thoughts.

High-intensity interval training (HIIT) is another effective method for combatting stress and overthinking. HIIT involves alternating between short bursts of intense exercise and brief rest periods. This form of workout improves physical fitness and has significant mental health benefits. HIIT releases endorphins and adrenaline, providing a natural mood boost and increasing energy levels. The intensity of HIIT workouts can distract you from overthinking, allowing you to focus on the immediate task rather than getting caught up in repetitive negative thoughts.

Dance therapy is a creative and engaging way to combat stress and overthinking through movement. Dancing allows self-expression, emotional release, and connection in a group setting. The rhythmic movements involved in dance can help regulate emotions and reduce feelings of anxiety by promoting a sense of flow and coordination between mind and body. Whether you prefer structured dance classes or simply dancing around your living room to your favorite tunes, incorporating dance into your routine can be a fun and effective way to break free from overthinking patterns.

Incorporating various exercises into your routine can provide holistic support for managing stress and overthinking. By exploring different types of physical activity, you can find what works best for you regarding both mental health benefits and enjoyment. Whether you choose to engage in cardiovascular workouts, strength training sessions, mind-body practices, HIIT sessions, dance therapy, or a combination of these modalities, prioritizing regular exercise is key to breaking free from the grips of overthinking and cultivating mental clarity.

Incorporating regular physical activity into your routine can be a powerful distraction from overthinking. Engaging in exercise benefits your physical health and plays a crucial role in improving your mental well-being. When caught in a cycle of intrusive thoughts, moving your body can help shift your focus away from rumination and towards the present moment.

Physical activity is a natural stress reliever, releasing endorphins that promote happiness and relaxation. These chemicals produced during exercise can counteract the negative effects of overthinking by boosting your mood and reducing anxiety levels. By making exercise a consistent part of your daily life, you create an opportunity to break free from the mental constraints often accompanying overthinking.

Choose activities that resonate with you, whether going for a brisk walk, practicing yoga, hitting the gym, or dancing to your favorite music. The key is to find something you enjoy that aligns with your preferences and lifestyle. Consistency is key in reaping the mental benefits of physical activity, so aim to incorporate movement into your routine regularly.

Physical activity serves as a productive outlet for pent-up energy and emotions, channeling them into constructive action rather than allowing them to fuel overthinking. When you exercise, you give your mind a break from the relentless stream of thoughts that may be causing distress or anxiety. This break can create space for clarity and perspective to emerge, helping you gain control over your mental state.

Consider incorporating mindfulness into your physical activities. Whether you're running, swimming, or practicing tai chi, being fully present in the moment can enhance the benefits of exercise for your mental well-being. Mindful movement allows you to connect with your body and surroundings, grounding you in the present and reducing the tendency to get lost in overthinking patterns.

Regular physical activity can improve sleep quality, often disrupted by overthinking and stress. By tiring out your body through exercise, you pave the way for more restful and rejuvenating sleep. Adequate rest is essential for mental clarity and emotional resilience, making physical activity a valuable tool for breaking free from the cycle of overthinking.

Incorporating variety into your workouts can keep things interesting and prevent monotony from setting in. Try different exercises or activities to challenge yourself physically and mentally while keeping boredom at bay. Experimenting with new forms of movement can also stimulate creativity and problem-solving skills, contributing to a more dynamic approach to managing overthinking tendencies.

Remember that progress takes time, so be patient with yourself as you integrate physical activity into your routine as a distraction from overthinking. Each step towards prioritizing movement and self-care brings you closer to cultivating mental clarity and emotional balance. Embrace the journey of incorporating regular exercise into your life as a powerful tool for breaking free from the grip of overthinking.

Understanding the intricate connection between physical activity and mental health is crucial for breaking the overthinking cycle and fostering mental clarity. By engaging in regular exercise, we enhance our physical well-being and create a robust defense against the persistent whirlwind of ruminative thoughts.

Physical activity is a powerful tool that interrupts the ongoing cycle of negative thinking, providing immediate relief and long-term benefits. Consistent exercise can activate your body's natural stress-relief mechanisms, improving mood and reducing anxiety. The variety of exercises discussed in this chapter—from brisk walking to yoga—offers each individual a way to find what best suits their lifestyle and preferences.

Incorporating these exercises into your daily routine can be a transformative strategy for managing stress. It's not just about distraction; it's about rechanneling your energy and focus towards activities that yield positive health outcomes. This shift alleviates the symptoms of overthinking and empowers you to regain control over your mental processes.

Embrace these practices with the understanding that you can master your mental landscape. Start small if you need to; even short periods of physical activity can significantly impact your mental clarity and emotional resilience. Remember, the goal is to build a sustainable habit that supports your mental health in the long term.

Let this knowledge act as a springboard for action. Take decisive steps towards integrating physical activity into your daily life, and observe its profound effects on your overall mental well-being. The power to change lies within you, and through these actionable strategies, you are well-equipped to foster a healthier, more balanced mind.

By actively engaging with these exercises, you are moving beyond the mind's confines and paving the way for a more serene and focused existence. Embrace this journey with confidence and optimism, knowing that each step you take is a move towards a more peaceful and empowered self.

Chapter 9: Recognizing Ruminative Routines

"Don't believe everything you think.

Thoughts are just that — thoughts."

Allan Lokos

Are You Stuck in Your Head?

Overthinking can feel like an endless loop, replaying the same worries and scenarios without resolution. This repetitive mental cycle drains energy and prevents you from enjoying life fully. Recognizing and addressing these ruminative routines is crucial, especially in specific contexts such as relationships, career decisions, and daily challenges. By tailoring strategies to these scenarios, you can break free from the mental fog and reclaim your clarity and peace.

Understanding Ruminative Thought Patterns

Ruminative thoughts are like unwanted guests who refuse to leave. They keep coming back, often focusing on negative outcomes or past mistakes. The first step to managing overthinking is identifying these patterns. Once you recognize them, you can see how they affect your mood and behavior across different aspects of your life. This awareness is the foundation for change, setting the stage for more specialized strategies that address the unique challenges of each situation.

Recognizing Triggers in Everyday Life

Every person has specific triggers that set off their spiral of overthinking. It could be a casual remark from a colleague or a minor setback in a personal project. Understanding what prompts your ruminative thoughts is a powerful tool. It allows you to prepare and respond proactively rather than getting swept away by the current of your own thoughts.

Shifting Focus Towards Constructive Thinking

Breaking free from negative thought cycles requires a shift towards more constructive thinking. This doesn't mean ignoring problems but approaching them with a solution-oriented mindset. By focusing on potential solutions rather than dwelling on the problems, you empower yourself to take actionable steps toward resolution and growth.

Strategies Tailored to Your Life

The effectiveness of any strategy depends on its relevance to your life. Strategies that work well in a relationship context might not be as effective when dealing with career-related overthinking. This chapter will explore how to customize approaches to fit seamlessly into your everyday life, enhancing their impact and usability.

Practical Steps for Immediate Relief

Immediate relief from overthinking is possible with simple yet effective techniques. These techniques interrupt ruminative thoughts and redirect attention towards more productive activities. Whether through mindfulness practices, physical activity, or structured problem-solving, these actions can provide quick relief while building long-term resilience against overthinking.

Empower Yourself Through Emotional Mastery

You have the innate ability to master your emotions and overcome mental clutter. By actively engaging with the strategies discussed, you can take charge of your mental space, turning obstacles into opportunities for personal growth and stability.

This chapter provides practical solutions tailored to the daily challenges, laying the groundwork for transforming how you handle overthinking with confidence and composure.

Identifying and understanding ruminative thought patterns is crucial in breaking free from the cycle of overthinking. Recognizing these patterns offers insight into your thought processes, shedding light on why certain thoughts loop endlessly. Overthinking is a common challenge; acknowledging it helps you know you're not alone.

By identifying your ruminative thought patterns, you unravel the causes behind your overthinking, often rooted in past experiences, fears about the future, or deep-seated beliefs about yourself. This understanding offers clarity on how to effectively address overthinking.

To identify ruminative thought patterns, observe recurring themes in your thoughts. Do you dwell on past mistakes or worry excessively about future outcomes? Recognizing these themes helps pinpoint triggers that lead to overthinking.

Understanding ruminative thought patterns also involves recognizing their impact on emotions and behaviors. Overthinking can heighten anxiety, indecision, and procrastination, perpetuating negative cycles. Awareness of its effects empowers you to break free from these patterns.

Developing self-awareness around ruminative thought patterns through mindfulness and reflection untangles the web of overthinking that may hinder personal growth. Clarifying your thought processes enables positive changes and cultivates a peaceful mind.

Recognizing triggers that fuel overthinking is essential. Awareness of specific contexts or events that provoke excessive thinking allows proactive intervention and redirection toward constructive thoughts. This awareness restores control over your mental processes.

Uncertainty often triggers overthinking. Ambiguous situations prompt endless speculation, increasing anxiety. Accepting uncertainty as an opportunity for growth mitigates overthinking's grip.

Perfectionism fuels overthinking by fixating on flawless outcomes. Embracing imperfection and setting realistic goals alleviates this pressure, fostering self-compassion.

Relationships, whether personal or professional, trigger overthinking through insecurities and doubts. Establishing boundaries and improving communication fosters healthier connections and emotional well-being.

High-pressure environments like work or academics intensify overthinking. Effective time management, prioritization, and stress reduction mitigate its impact, enhancing resilience.

Daily setbacks prompt overthinking by fixating on failures. Embracing setbacks as learning opportunities build resilience and a growth mindset focused on progress.

External factors such as media and social comparison amplify overthinking. Setting boundaries, prioritizing self-care, and practicing mindfulness restore mental clarity amid constant stimuli.

In summary, recognizing overthinking triggers empowers proactive intervention. Understanding contexts that fuel rumination enables targeted strategies and redirects focus to constructive thoughts.

Practical strategies are crucial to shift from negative to constructive thoughts. Mindfulness fosters an objective perspective amid challenges. Cognitive restructuring reframes negative thinking, promoting a balanced mindset.

Gratitude journaling cultivates positivity by appreciating life's blessings daily. Physical activity releases endorphins, reducing stress and enhancing mental clarity, whether through yoga or gym sessions.

Setting realistic goals celebrates progress and sustains positive thinking. Seeking social support offers new perspectives and emotional validation, fostering resilience.

Self-care practices like reading or nature walks recharge energy and refocus attention positively. These strategies consistently cultivate resilience against negative thought patterns, fostering constructive thinking.

Understanding thought intricacies enhances mental clarity amid ruminative cycles. Tailoring coping mechanisms to specific contexts optimizes effectiveness in managing challenges.

Actionable steps redirect mental energy. Applying techniques like mindfulness or problem-solving enhances adaptability. Managing responses to negative thoughts builds resilience and reduces anxiety.

Mastering your mental landscape involves understanding and managing thoughts for a clearer mind. Consistent engagement with strategies transforms thought relationships and enhances life.

Each situation offers learning and growth opportunities. Embracing problem-solving and self-reflection reclaims mental control. Persistence in shifting focus from worry to clarity fosters peace and personal growth.

Chapter 10: Contextual Conquests

"To understand the immeasurable, the mind

must be extraordinarily quiet, still."

Jiddu Krishnamurti

Unravel the Chains: How Stopping Overthinking Strengthens Connections and Sharpens Decisions

In our journey through the labyrinth of mental clarity, we often stumble upon the intricate trap of overthinking. This excessive mental churn clouds judgment and weakens our interpersonal relationships and professional efficacy. By learning to arrest this cycle, you can enhance your ability to connect with others and make decisions with confidence and speed. This chapter delves into practical strategies tailored to refine your thinking patterns, enriching your personal and professional lives.

Overthinking is a common obstacle that impedes progress in various aspects of life. Whether it's a personal relationship or a career decision, the inability to move past incessant thoughts can lead to stagnation and distress. Here, we explore tailored strategies that help mitigate overthinking by adapting them to specific life contexts. Understanding when and where to apply these techniques can significantly improve how you interact and respond in different situations.

Moreover, relationships and workplace environments often suffer under the weight of indecisive actions bred by overthinking. Practicing practical advice can cultivate healthier relationships and a more productive work atmosphere. This involves recognizing patterns of overthinking that specifically affect these areas and addressing them directly with effective mental tools.

Daily setbacks are inevitable, but how we handle these challenges can define our path. Adjusting your mental approach during these times is crucial for maintaining emotional balance and making sound decisions. This segment will focus on customizing cognitive techniques to better manage everyday challenges, thus preventing them from escalating into larger issues.

The capacity to master one's mental processes dictates personal success and how effectively one navigates through life's myriad interactions. Each section of this chapter builds upon the last, forming a comprehensive guide designed to equip you with the necessary tools for overcoming the barriers posed by overthinking.

Empower yourself by embracing these techniques, understanding their relevance in different scenarios, and applying them consistently. The goal is straightforward: transform overthinking from a hindrance into an opportunity for growth and learning. With each step forward, you reclaim a piece of your mental peace and operational efficiency.

Remember, the journey toward mental clarity is not about suppressing thoughts but channeling them constructively. As you progress through this chapter, you will be better equipped to engage more meaningfully and effectively with the world around you. Let's embark on this path together, fostering connections that thrive on clarity and decisions that reflect true confidence.

Tailoring strategies to specific life situations is crucial in navigating the intricate web of overthinking. Each scenario we encounter brings its own set of challenges and triggers for overthinking. By customizing our approach to different contexts, we can effectively address the root causes of our excessive thoughts and find tailored solutions that work best for us. Whether unraveling the complexities of relationships, facing work demands, or dealing with daily setbacks, adapting our strategies can lead to more effective outcomes and a sense of control over our mental processes.

Whether romantic, familial, or social, relationships often serve as fertile ground for overthinking. In these intimate spaces, our vulnerabilities are exposed, triggering a cascade of doubts and anxieties. To navigate this terrain successfully, it's essential to communicate openly and honestly with our partners or loved ones. Establishing clear boundaries, expressing needs and concerns, and actively listening can help alleviate misunderstandings that fuel relationship overthinking. Additionally, practicing mindfulness and staying present in interactions can foster deeper connections and reduce the tendency to dwell on hypothetical scenarios.

Work environments present unique challenges that can exacerbate overthinking tendencies. The pressure to perform, make decisions quickly, or navigate office politics can be overwhelming. Setting realistic goals and priorities is key to combating overthinking at work. Breaking tasks into manageable steps, seeking clarification when needed, and learning to delegate responsibilities can prevent feeling overwhelmed by endless thoughts related to work tasks. Moreover, practicing self-compassion and acknowledging one's efforts rather than fixating on perceived shortcomings can foster a healthier mindset in professional settings.

Daily setbacks are inevitable in life, but how we respond to them can perpetuate or break the cycle of overthinking. Reframing negative thoughts into more constructive narratives is essential when faced with obstacles or disappointments. Cultivating resilience by focusing on solutions rather than problems can empower individuals to overcome setbacks with grace and determination. Embracing self-care practices such as exercise, meditation, or engaging in hobbies can also provide much-needed respite from persistent overthinking caused by daily stressors.

Tailoring strategies to specific life situations empowers individuals to confront their overthinking tendencies head-on. By customizing approaches for relationships, work environments, and daily setbacks, individuals can cultivate a sense of agency over their mental processes and forge a path toward greater clarity and peace of mind.

In relationships and work, overthinking can be particularly detrimental, clouding our judgment and hindering our ability to connect authentically with others or make sound decisions. Navigating these spheres with a clear mind and focused perspective is crucial for fostering healthy relationships and achieving professional success. Let's explore some practical strategies to help you manage overthinking in these key areas of your life.

Overcoming Overthinking in Relationships

Regarding relationships, overthinking can sow seeds of doubt and create unnecessary tension. One effective strategy is to practice active listening. Instead of getting lost in your thoughts during conversations, consciously listen to what the other person is saying. This can help you stay present in the moment and foster a deeper connection.

Building Trust Through Communication

Open and honest communication is another powerful tool for combating overthinking in relationships. Instead of making assumptions or jumping to conclusions, have candid conversations with your partner or loved ones. Express your thoughts and feelings clearly, and encourage them to do the same. This transparency can help build trust and reduce the need for excessive rumination.

Managing Overthinking at Work

In the professional sphere, overthinking can lead to indecision, procrastination, and decreased productivity. To combat this, set realistic goals and prioritize tasks. Break down complex projects into manageable steps, focusing on one task at a time. Creating a clear action plan can alleviate the feeling of being overwhelmed and boost your efficiency.

Embracing Mindfulness in the Workplace

Practicing mindfulness can also be immensely beneficial in managing overthinking at work. Take short breaks throughout the day to center yourself and refocus your mind. Engage in deep breathing exercises or brief meditation sessions to calm your thoughts. By incorporating moments of mindfulness into your workday, you can enhance your concentration and reduce mental clutter.

Seeking Feedback and Support

Don't be afraid to seek feedback from colleagues or supervisors. Constructive input can provide valuable insights and help you gain perspective on your work. Additionally, reaching out for support when needed can prevent isolation and alleviate the burden of overthinking.

Implementing Boundaries

In both personal relationships and professional settings, it's essential to establish boundaries that protect your mental well-being. Learn to say no when necessary, prioritize self-care, and set aside time for relaxation and rejuvenation. Honoring your boundaries can prevent burnout and maintain a healthy balance between work and personal life.

Taking Action Today

Remember, managing to overthink in relationships and at work requires proactive steps. By practicing active listening, fostering open communication, setting goals, embracing mindfulness, seeking feedback, establishing boundaries, and prioritizing self-care, you can cultivate healthier relationships, enhance your productivity at work, and experience greater peace of mind overall.

Embrace these strategies as tools in your arsenal against overthinking—empower yourself to navigate relationships with clarity and approach work challenges confidently. Taking decisive action today paves the way for more meaningful connections, increased productivity, and a more balanced approach to life.

Adjusting techniques to suit daily setbacks and decision-making processes is crucial in maintaining progress and momentum in overcoming overthinking. When faced with unexpected challenges or setbacks, it's important to have strategies to navigate these moments effectively. One key approach is practicing mindfulness, which involves staying present and acknowledging thoughts without judgment. By focusing on the current situation rather than getting lost in future scenarios or past regrets, individuals can reduce the impact of overthinking on their daily lives.

Another valuable technique is establishing a routine that includes time for reflection and relaxation. Setting aside dedicated moments for self-care, such as meditation, exercise, or simply walking in nature, can help manage stress and prevent overthinking from spiraling out of control. Consistency in these activities is key to reaping their benefits fully.

When it comes to decision-making, it's essential to balance gathering information and taking action. Overthinkers often get caught up in endless analysis without reaching a conclusion. By setting deadlines for decisions and weighing the pros and cons efficiently, individuals can avoid getting stuck in a cycle of overthinking that hampers progress. Creating a decision-making framework based on priorities and values can also streamline the process and provide clarity when faced with tough choices.

In moments of uncertainty or doubt, seeking advice from trusted friends or mentors is helpful. External perspectives can offer fresh insights and help overthinkers see situations from different angles, potentially breaking through mental roadblocks. However, balancing external input with personal intuition and judgment is crucial to making decisions that align with individual goals and values.

Lastly, practicing self-compassion is vital when adjusting techniques for daily setbacks. Overcoming overthinking is not linear; setbacks are natural occurrences on the path to mental clarity. Being gentle with oneself during challenging times can foster resilience and motivate continued progress toward breaking free from the grips of overthinking.

In summary, adapting techniques to manage daily setbacks and decision-making processes requires a combination of mindfulness, routine establishment, balanced decision-making approaches, seeking external advice when needed, and practicing self-compassion throughout the journey. By consistently incorporating these strategies into daily life, individuals can gradually reduce the impact of overthinking on their well-being and cultivate a more grounded and confident approach to navigating challenges.

Throughout this chapter, we have explored how tailoring overthinking strategies to specific life scenarios can profoundly impact your mental clarity and overall well-being. Applying these customized strategies in your personal relationships and workplace enables you to engage more genuinely with others and make decisions with increased confidence and efficiency.

It is crucial to recognize that each situation in life demands a distinct approach to managing overthinking. Whether you're navigating daily setbacks or facing significant decisions, the ability to adjust your mental processes is a powerful tool. This adaptability enhances your interactions and bolsters your professional performance, proving that mastering your mind is both a personal triumph and a practical advantage.

Remember, the journey to overcoming overthinking is deeply personal but universally relevant. You are not alone in this challenge; the strategies discussed here are designed to be accessible and actionable. Embrace these techniques with the understanding that you can control your thoughts and, consequently, shape your life's outcomes.

As you move forward, I encourage you to actively apply these insights. Each step taken is a step towards a more present and fulfilling life. Harness these strategies to break free from overthinking and embrace a future where calm and clarity define your days.

Chapter 11: Decision Dynamics

"Sometimes the most important thing in a whole day

is the rest we take between two deep breaths."

Etty Hillesum

From Overthinking to Overcoming: Harness the Power of Decisive Action

When caught in the relentless whirl of overthinking, making even the simplest decision can feel daunting. This paralysis by analysis not only saps your mental energy but also blocks the path to personal and professional growth. However, there is a transformative approach that can shift your mental gears from passive rumination to dynamic problem-solving. By learning to stop overthinking, you enhance your decision-making capabilities, paving the way for a clearer, more assertive mind.

Embrace Clarity, Enhance Decision-Making

The first key item we will explore is the direct correlation between reducing overthinking and improving decision-making. Overthinkers often find themselves trapped in a maze of "what ifs" and worst-case scenarios, leading to decision fatigue and a significant drain on emotional well-being. By adopting strategies that curtail this cycle, you not only free up mental space but also enable quicker, more confident decisions. This shift is crucial for personal satisfaction and leveraging opportunities that require timely action.

Clear-headedness: A Catalyst for Better Relationships

Secondly, we delve into how clarity of thought directly influences interpersonal relationships. Overthinking can cloud judgment and foster misunderstandings in communication. Promoting a mindset focused on clear and present thinking can improve your interactions with others. This not only enhances personal relationships but also strengthens professional connections, creating a network of support that is based on mutual respect and understanding.

Strategies for Proactive Living

Lastly, we will cover practical strategies to foster decisiveness and a proactive approach to daily challenges. Transitioning from a passive observer to an active participant in your life involves setting small, achievable goals that encourage forward momentum. Each step taken is a building block in constructing a resilient mindset capable of tackling complex problems with ease and confidence.

Empowerment through Action

Empowering yourself to take decisive action is not just about combating indecision; it's about reclaiming control over your mental landscape. The techniques discussed are designed not only to break the cycle of overthinking but also to instill a habit of proactive problem-solving that stands strong in the face of stress and anxiety.

Understanding Your Potential

You must recognize that you possess the innate ability to master your thoughts and steer them toward productive outcomes. Embracing this power can transform how you perceive challenges—viewing them as opportunities rather than obstacles.

Practical Steps Forward

The journey from overthinking to effective decision-making involves practical steps that are both manageable and measurable. By implementing these strategies consistently, you pave the way for sustained mental clarity and an enhanced sense of control over your life's direction.

As we progress through these themes, remember that each concept is a stepping stone towards building a clearer mind and a more fulfilling life. The tools provided are designed to be immediately applicable, offering relief from the burdens of overanalysis and pathways toward richer, more engaging experiences across all facets of life.

Cultivating Clear-Headedness to Enhance Interpersonal Relationships

Overthinking can often hinder our decision-making process, leading to indecision and overwhelm. The constant loop of thoughts can cloud our judgment and make it challenging to see the best path forward clearly. By learning to stop overthinking, we can significantly improve our decision-making skills and cultivate a more proactive approach to problem-solving.

One key aspect of halting overthinking is recognizing when we are stuck in this cycle. Awareness is the first step towards change. When we ruminate excessively on a particular issue or scenario, we must pause and acknowledge that overthinking occurs. This self-awareness allows us to break free from the grip of endless thoughts and begin shifting toward a more decisive mindset.

To enhance decision-making, it's crucial to focus on actionable outcomes rather than getting lost in hypothetical scenarios. By setting clear goals and identifying achievable steps to reach them, we can direct our energy towards constructive problem-solving. Breaking down complex decisions into manageable tasks can make the process less daunting and more attainable.

Another strategy to improve decision-making is practicing mindfulness. Mindfulness involves staying present in the moment without judgment, which can help quiet the noise of overthinking and bring clarity to our thoughts. By cultivating mindfulness, we can approach decisions with a calmer and more focused mind, enabling us to make choices based on rationality rather than emotions or excessive analysis.

Embracing a proactive mindset is also instrumental in breaking free from overthinking patterns. Instead of waiting for solutions to come to us, taking the initiative and seeking out information or advice can empower us to make informed decisions. Proactivity shifts our perspective from a passive stance of rumination to an active role in shaping our outcomes.

Interpersonal relationships are crucial in our lives, influencing our emotions, behaviors, and overall well-being. These relationships can become strained when grappling with overthinking, as the constant barrage of thoughts can cloud our interactions with others. However, we can navigate these relationships more effectively and authentically by attaining clear-headedness. Clear-headedness allows us to communicate openly, listen actively, and empathize genuinely with those around us.

One significant benefit of achieving clarity in our thoughts is engaging fully in conversations. When we are not consumed by overthinking, we can be present in the moment, actively participating in discussions and truly connecting with others. This presence fosters deeper connections and promotes understanding within relationships. By being fully engaged, we show respect and consideration for the people we interact with, creating a more positive and fulfilling social environment.

Another advantage of clear-headedness in interpersonal relationships is the capacity to resolve conflicts effectively. Overthinkers often struggle with conflicts as their minds become entangled in endless negative thoughts and scenarios. When we approach conflicts clearly, we can address issues directly, express our feelings assertively, and seek mutually beneficial solutions. This proactive stance resolves conflicts more efficiently and strengthens bonds by demonstrating honesty and vulnerability.

Empathy is a cornerstone of healthy relationships, fostering understanding, compassion, and connection. Overthinking can hinder our ability to empathize fully with others, as it distracts us from their emotions and experiences. With a clear mind, we can attune ourselves to the feelings of those around us, offering support, validation, and kindness when needed. This heightened empathy deepens our relationships and cultivates trust and intimacy with others.

In addition to enhancing communication, conflict resolution, and empathy, clear-headedness promotes authenticity in interpersonal relationships. Overthinkers may struggle to authentically express their thoughts and emotions due to fear of judgment or rejection. By embracing mental clarity, individuals can communicate openly and honestly with others, sharing their genuine selves without reservation. This authenticity builds trust and intimacy within relationships, creating a space for vulnerability and emotional connection.

Ultimately, clear-headedness empowers individuals to engage meaningfully in their interpersonal relationships by fostering presence, effective communication, conflict resolution skills, empathy, and authenticity. Individuals can nurture strong bonds with others based on mutual respect, understanding, and genuine connection by cultivating mental clarity. This transformation enriches personal relationships and contributes to overall emotional well-being and fulfillment in social interactions.

Decision-Making Clarity Framework

The Decision-Making Clarity Framework is a structured model designed to streamline decision-making processes and mitigate the effects of overthinking. This framework comprises four key components: Situation Analysis, Option Generation, Risk Assessment, and Decision Execution. Each component is crucial in guiding individuals toward making informed and confident decisions, ultimately breaking the cycle of overthinking and indecision.

Situation Analysis

In the Situation Analysis stage, individuals are encouraged to gather relevant information and comprehensively understand the decision's context. This step involves thoroughly examining the factors, identifying key stakeholders, and assessing any constraints or limitations that may impact the decision-making process. By employing tools like SWOT analysis (Strengths, Weaknesses, Opportunities, Threats), individuals can gain valuable insights into their current situation and lay a solid foundation for moving forward with clarity.

Option Generation

Option Generation focuses on brainstorming potential courses of action without passing judgment on their feasibility or desirability. This stage encourages creativity and open-mindedness, allowing individuals to explore various possibilities without feeling constrained by preconceived notions. By generating multiple options, individuals can expand their perspectives and consider alternative solutions that may not have been initially apparent.

Risk Assessment

The risk assessment phase evaluates each option's potential outcomes and cons. Individuals are prompted to weigh the pros and cons of each alternative, considering factors such as feasibility, impact, and alignment with their goals and values. Employing techniques such as creating pros-and-cons lists can help individuals clarify their thoughts and make more informed decisions based on a thorough analysis of the risks involved.

Decision Execution

Decision Execution marks the final stage of the framework, where individuals select the most suitable option based on their analysis in the previous steps. This phase involves committing to a course of action, outlining specific steps for implementation, and setting a timeline for execution. By taking decisive action and following through on their chosen plan, individuals can overcome hesitation and move forward with confidence, breaking free from the paralysis of overthinking.

The Decision-Making Clarity Framework operates as an integrated system where each component interacts synergistically to guide individuals toward effective decision-making. By following this structured approach, individuals can navigate complex situations with clarity and purpose, leading to more decisive actions and positive outcomes in both personal and professional spheres.

In this chapter, we've navigated through the transformative journey from passive overthinking to active problem-solving. By understanding how halting the cycle of overthinking enhances decision-making, you can now appreciate the pivotal role of clear-headedness in strengthening interpersonal relationships. Moreover, the strategies discussed to foster decisiveness and proactivity are your tools to cope and thrive.

Stopping overthinking is crucial. It liberates your mind, allowing you to make decisions with confidence and clarity. This clarity isn't just beneficial in isolation; it extends to how you interact with others. Clear communication and empathy are bolstered when your mind is uncluttered by needless worries.

The benefits of clear-headedness in relationships are profound. It fosters a deeper connection and understanding between individuals, paving the way for more meaningful and supportive interactions. This isn't just theory; it's a practical outcome of applying the principles of mental clarity.

To transform your thought processes, employ strategies promoting decisiveness and proactivity. These are abstract concepts and real, actionable steps you can implement today. Whether setting small, achievable goals or challenging negative thought patterns, each action is a step towards a more controlled and fulfilling mental state.

Remember, the shift from passive rumination to active problem-solving doesn't just alleviate stress—it enhances your overall sense of control and accomplishment. You're not merely avoiding negative thoughts; you're actively constructing a positive framework for your mental health.

Embrace these changes with the understanding that each step forward is a building block in mastering your mind. This proactive approach isn't just about solving problems as they arise; it's about reshaping your mental landscape to prevent overthinking from reoccurring.

By implementing these strategies, you equip yourself with the tools to navigate life's challenges more effectively. Let this knowledge empower you as you continue to unlock mental clarity, embrace calm, and leave overthinking and anxiety behind. Take control of your thoughts, and watch as new possibilities unfold in your personal and professional life.

Chapter 12: Problem-Solving Prodigies

"The thing about meditation is you

become more and more you."

David Lynch

Transform Your Thoughts: From Overthinking to Overcoming

The journey to mental clarity is often obstructed by the habitual maze of overthinking—a common trap for many who strive for personal and professional success. Recognizing this, we delve into strategies that alleviate the burden of excessive contemplation and transform it into a constructive problem-solving prowess. This approach fosters resilience and encourages a proactive stance towards life's challenges.

Embracing a Proactive Problem-Solving Approach

Overthinkers typically get caught in analysis paralysis, where decisions seem daunting and progress stalls. The first transformative strategy focuses on replacing these tendencies with a proactive approach to problem-solving. This means learning to identify core issues quickly and applying practical solutions without dwelling excessively on possible outcomes. Doing so empowers you to take decisive action, paving the way for clearer thought processes and reduced anxiety.

Setting Achievable Goals

Another vital component is the setting of achievable goals. These goals act as stepping stones that guide your journey towards mental clarity, providing clear markers of your progress and boosting your confidence with each accomplishment. By breaking down larger objectives into smaller, manageable tasks, you can maintain motivation and avoid the overwhelming flood of concerns that often leads to overthinking.

Cultivating an Action-Oriented Mindset

Developing an action-oriented mindset is perhaps the most crucial step in overcoming overthinking. This mindset emphasizes doing over pondering, pushing you towards direct engagement with your problems rather than merely contemplating them. It's about cultivating a can-do attitude and prioritizing effective action over perfect plans.

Why These Strategies Matter

For those trapped in cycles of overthinking, these strategies are not just methods but essential tools for rebuilding their mental framework. They offer a structured way to navigate the fog of thoughts that cloud judgment and impede action. Importantly, they also promote mental resilience, equipping individuals with the capacity to handle future challenges with greater agility and confidence.

By adopting these approaches, overthinkers can transform their inherent analytical skills into a powerful asset—turning what once hindered them into a key component of their success strategy. This shift enhances personal productivity and contributes significantly to emotional well-being.

The Path Forward

As we explore these themes further in this chapter, remember that each strategy is designed to be accessible and actionable. The emphasis is always on practical application—providing you with tools that can be immediately implemented to see tangible improvements in your mental clarity and overall quality of life.

Through understanding and applying these principles, you are taking control of your mental landscape, turning barriers into bridges towards a clearer, more focused existence. It's about moving from passive worry to active engagement in creating a life characterized by emotional mastery and fulfillment.

Overthinking can often feel like a never-ending loop of thoughts, trapping individuals in a cycle of indecision and anxiety. However, embracing a proactive approach to problem-solving can serve as a powerful antidote to this mental struggle. Instead of getting lost in a maze of overanalyzing every detail, shifting focus towards taking action is essential. By proactively addressing issues as they arise, you can prevent them from snowballing into overwhelming problems.

One key strategy is to break down larger tasks into smaller, more manageable steps. This approach makes daunting challenges seem less intimidating and allows for a sense of progress and accomplishment along the way. Rather than being paralyzed by the enormity of a situation, tackling it piece by piece can instill a sense of control and empowerment.

Another valuable technique is to prioritize tasks based on urgency and importance. By identifying what needs immediate attention versus what can wait, you can streamline your efforts and avoid feeling overwhelmed by trying to do everything at once. This targeted approach helps channel your energy effectively towards resolving issues without getting lost in unnecessary details.

Moreover, adopting a solution-focused mindset can help reframe how you approach problems. Instead of dwelling on the negatives or potential obstacles, focus on finding practical solutions. This shift in perspective encourages active problem-solving rather than passive rumination. By training your mind to seek solutions, you cultivate a habit of taking decisive action rather than getting stuck in endless analysis.

Setting achievable goals is a crucial step in breaking free from the cycle of overthinking. Individuals can create a roadmap towards progress and success by establishing clear and attainable objectives. It is essential to start with small, manageable, easily accomplished goals. These initial victories provide a sense of achievement and motivate further action. Remember, progress is progress, no matter how small it may seem.

When setting goals, it is important to be specific. Vague aspirations can lead to confusion and lack of direction. Define your objectives clearly, outlining the steps needed to reach them. This clarity not only guides your actions but also enhances focus and determination. Each goal should be measurable, allowing you to track progress and celebrate milestones.

Another key aspect of goal-setting is relevance. Ensure that your objectives align with your overall vision and values. Goals that resonate with your aspirations will likely keep you motivated and engaged. Consider the significance of each goal and your long-term ambitions, adjusting them if necessary to stay on course.

Moreover, make your goals time-bound. Setting deadlines creates a sense of urgency and helps prevent procrastination. Establish a timeline for each objective, breaking down larger tasks into manageable chunks with specific completion dates. This approach boosts productivity and instills a sense of discipline and commitment.

In addition to being realistic, goals should be challenging enough to inspire growth and development. Striking a balance between achievability and stretch encourages you to push beyond your comfort zone while maintaining a sense of feasibility. Embrace challenges as opportunities for learning and improvement, embracing the process rather than fixating solely on outcomes.

As you progress towards your goals, remember to celebrate your achievements, no matter how small they may seem. Acknowledge your efforts and the progress you have made, reinforcing a positive mindset and boosting self-confidence. Each step forward is a testament to your dedication and perseverance in overcoming overthinking patterns.

In conclusion, setting achievable goals that promote a sense of accomplishment is a powerful strategy for combating overthinking tendencies. Individuals can cultivate resilience and motivation in their problem-solving journey by defining clear objectives, staying focused, aligning goals with values, establishing deadlines, and balancing realism with challenge. Celebrating successes along the way reinforces positive thinking patterns and nurtures a proactive mindset essential for mental well-being.

Developing an action-oriented mindset is crucial to foster mental resilience and combat the challenges of overthinking. Taking proactive steps towards addressing overthinking tendencies can significantly improve mental well-being and overall quality of life. Instead of dwelling on thoughts endlessly, engaging in purposeful actions can shift focus away from rumination and towards productive problem-solving. By embracing an action-oriented approach, individuals can cultivate a sense of empowerment and control over their thoughts and emotions.

Setting clear objectives and breaking them into manageable tasks is a powerful way to develop an action-oriented mindset. Individuals can track progress and celebrate small victories by creating a roadmap for achieving goals. This boosts motivation and instills a sense of accomplishment, reinforcing the belief that proactive steps lead to tangible results.

In the journey towards mental resilience, it is essential to cultivate a habit of taking decisive actions even in the face of uncertainty or discomfort. Procrastination and indecisiveness often fuel overthinking, leading to increased stress and anxiety. By making intentional choices and committing to follow through, individuals can build confidence in their ability to overcome challenges.

Embracing a "do it now" mentality can be transformative in combating overthinking tendencies. Instead of allowing thoughts to linger and escalate, taking immediate action on tasks or decisions can prevent unnecessary rumination. This proactive approach not only reduces mental clutter but also instills a sense of control over one's thoughts and reactions.

To foster mental resilience, it is crucial to practice self-compassion when faced with setbacks or challenges. Developing an action-oriented mindset does not mean expecting perfection but embracing growth and learning. Individuals can navigate obstacles with resilience and determination by treating themselves with kindness and understanding.

Focusing on progress rather than perfection is essential in cultivating an action-oriented mindset. Individuals can build momentum toward lasting change by recognizing that every step taken toward overcoming overthinking is valuable. Celebrating small wins and learning from setbacks are integral to the journey towards mental resilience.

By adopting an action-oriented mindset, individuals can empower themselves to take control of their thoughts and emotions. Through consistent practice and dedication to proactive problem-solving, it is possible to break free from the cycle of overthinking and cultivate a sense of mental clarity and resilience.

Embracing a Proactive Approach

The journey toward mental clarity and resilience begins with a proactive approach to problem-solving. By choosing action over passive worry, you empower yourself to construct a path forward, transforming overthinking into a blueprint for success. This shift alleviates the stress associated with inaction and fosters a sense of control over your mental landscape.

Setting Achievable Goals

Goal setting is fundamental in building confidence and maintaining momentum in facing challenges. Establishing clear, achievable goals provides a series of victories that propel you forward and reinforce your capability to manage and overcome obstacles. Remember, each small achievement is a step towards mastering your mental environment.

Cultivating an Action-Oriented Mindset

Developing an action-oriented mindset is crucial for sustained mental health and resilience. This mindset encourages continuous engagement with your goals and challenges, ensuring you remain active, adaptive, and responsive to life's complexities. It's about committing to move forward, regardless of your obstacles.

Empowerment through Positive Frameworks

Integrating motivational elements and frameworks that promote a growth mindset is not just beneficial; it's transformative. These tools help in reframing challenges as opportunities, enabling you to navigate through moments of doubt with greater ease and confidence. Leveraging positive narratives and success stories can significantly bolster your resilience, providing clear examples of what's possible when you apply these principles in your own life.

Action Over Anxiety

By adopting these strategies, you're not merely coping with

overthinking and anxiety but actively overcoming them. It's about taking control and using the tools to forge a path toward surviving and thriving. Engage with these practices regularly, and your capacity for handling stress and anxiety grows stronger daily.

Remember, overcoming overthinking and embracing calm is within your reach. Applying these actionable insights means you're on your way to unlocking a more peaceful and empowered state of mind. Start today and take a significant step toward a life characterized by mental clarity and emotional resilience.

Chapter 13: The Motivational Mindset

"Our life is shaped by our mind, for we

become what we think."

Buddha

Harness the Power of a Motivational Mindset to Break Free from Overthinking

Motivation is the backbone of persistence; even the most potent strategies can fall short without it. This chapter addresses why integrating motivational content is not merely an option but necessary for those seeking to consistently manage their thoughts. We will explore practical ways to infuse daily thought practices with inspiring insights that keep you committed to your mental health goals.

Furthermore, adopting a positive thinking framework is crucial for mental growth. It's not enough to push away negative thoughts; one must also actively cultivate positivity. This section will introduce effective and easy frameworks to integrate into everyday life, ensuring that positive thinking becomes more than just a practice—it becomes a habit.

Success stories and relatable scenarios form the third pillar of this chapter, providing concrete examples of how effective thought management can dramatically improve one's quality of life. These narratives are not just stories but proof that the strategies discussed work in real-life contexts. They serve as both inspiration and instruction, offering a roadmap to those who might feel lost in their mental mazes.

This chapter aims to make learning enjoyable and engaging by employing a conversational tone and incorporating humor where appropriate. Understanding that each reader's journey is unique, the content is designed to be adaptable, allowing individuals to tailor the strategies to fit their specific needs and circumstances.

It's essential to approach this topic with compassion and empathy, recognizing that the struggle with overthinking is both common and challenging. The aim is to inform and empower readers, giving them the tools to reclaim control over their thoughts and emotions.

The strategies here are practical and actionable, designed for immediate application. This chapter ensures readers feel equipped and ready to implement these techniques daily by simplifying complex concepts into clear, concise language.

Through motivational insights, positive frameworks, and success stories, this chapter provides a comprehensive guide for anyone looking to break free from the cycle of overthinking and embrace a clearer, more focused mindset. It's about taking control, step by step, with confidence and clarity.

In the journey to combat overthinking, persistence is key. Integrating motivational content can be a powerful tool in inspiring individuals to manage their thoughts effectively. Motivation is the driving force that propels individuals forward, even when faced with challenges or setbacks. It instills a sense of purpose and determination, reminding individuals of the importance of their mental well-being and the transformative impact it can have on their lives.

Motivational content is a beacon of encouragement, illuminating the path toward mental clarity and emotional freedom. Highlighting success stories, practical strategies, and relatable anecdotes reminds individuals that change is possible and achievable. It instills hope and belief in one's ability to overcome obstacles and break free from the shackles of overthinking.

Embracing a motivational mindset fosters resilience in the face of adversity. It encourages individuals to view setbacks as opportunities for growth rather than insurmountable barriers. By internalizing a positive outlook and unwavering determination, individuals can navigate the complexities of their thoughts with grace and fortitude.

Motivational content acts as a catalyst for transformation, sparking a shift in perspective and empowering individuals to take control of their mental well-being. It inspires a proactive approach to thought management, urging individuals to engage actively with strategies and techniques that promote mental clarity and emotional balance.

Harnessing Positive Thinking Frameworks for Mental Growth

Positive thinking frameworks are pivotal in nurturing mental growth and fostering a resilient mindset. By implementing these frameworks, individuals can shift their perspectives towards more constructive and optimistic outlooks, improving emotional well-being and enhancing problem-solving abilities.

One effective strategy is the practice of gratitude. Taking time each day to reflect on gratitude can significantly impact overall mood and mindset. By acknowledging the positive aspects of life, even amidst challenges, individuals can cultivate a sense of abundance and contentment. This simple yet powerful exercise can help reframe negative thoughts and promote a more positive approach to daily experiences.

Another valuable framework involves affirmations. Affirmations are positive statements individuals repeat to themselves to challenge and overcome self-sabotaging beliefs. Individuals can reprogram their subconscious minds towards success and self-acceptance by consciously choosing empowering phrases that resonate with personal goals and values. Regularly incorporating affirmations into daily routines can reinforce confidence and optimism.

Visualization is also a potent tool for cultivating a positive mindset. By vividly imagining desired outcomes and success scenarios, individuals can harness the power of their imagination to manifest their aspirations. Visualization techniques can help reduce anxiety, increase motivation, and enhance focus towards achieving goals. Engaging in visualization exercises regularly can strengthen belief in one's capabilities and amplify motivation for taking proactive steps towards personal growth.

Embracing a growth mindset is fundamental for mental development. Cultivating the belief that abilities can be developed through dedication and hard work fosters resilience and perseverance in facing challenges. Viewing failures as opportunities for learning and growth rather than setbacks paves the way for continuous improvement and innovation. Encouraging oneself to embrace challenges as stepping stones toward personal evolution nurtures a sense of curiosity, adaptability, and grit.

Incorporating these positive thinking frameworks into daily routines can serve as pillars of support during challenging times, empowering individuals to navigate obstacles with grace and determination. By fostering an optimistic outlook grounded in gratitude, affirmations, visualization, and a growth mindset, individuals can cultivate resilience, nurture mental well-being, and unlock their full potential for personal growth and fulfillment.

By consistently embracing these strategies, individuals can lay a strong foundation for mental clarity, emotional balance, and sustainable progress toward leading fulfilling lives free from overthinking. Through intentional practice and dedication to nurturing a positive mindset, individuals can embark on a transformative journey toward self-discovery, empowerment, and inner peace.

Success stories and scenarios are powerful tools to illustrate the effectiveness of thought management strategies. By showcasing real-life examples of individuals who have successfully combated overthinking, readers can see tangible evidence that change is possible. These stories highlight the transformative power of implementing practical techniques and inspire those seeking to overcome mental hurdles.

One such scenario involves Sarah, a working professional overwhelmed by constant self-doubt and anxiety. Through consistent mindfulness practice and positive affirmations, Sarah gradually shifted her mindset from one plagued by negativity to one focused on self-empowerment and confidence. Sarah's journey serves as a testament to the impact of perseverance and dedication in reshaping thought patterns.

Another success story follows Mark, who struggled with intrusive thoughts that hindered his ability to concentrate at work. By engaging in cognitive behavioral therapy and journaling exercises, Mark learned to effectively challenge and reframe his negative thoughts. Mark's experience underscores the importance of seeking professional guidance and actively participating in strategies tailored to individual needs.

These examples demonstrate the potential for transformation and provide practical insights into the steps taken to achieve mental clarity. By following these narratives, readers can glean valuable lessons on resilience, adaptability, and the power of self-reflection in managing overthinking tendencies.

Furthermore, success stories offer hope and encouragement to individuals grappling with similar challenges. Knowing that others have faced similar struggles and emerged stronger on the other side can instill a sense of solidarity and motivation. These accounts remind readers that they are not alone in their journey toward mastering their thoughts.

In exploring various success stories, readers can identify with different aspects of each narrative and extract relevant strategies to apply in their own lives. The diversity of experiences showcased underscores the universal nature of overthinking struggles while highlighting individuals' unique paths to achieve mental clarity.

By delving into these success stories and scenarios, readers are invited to envision their own potential for growth and change. The relatability of these accounts fosters a sense of connection and understanding, reinforcing the belief that with dedication and perseverance, it is possible to break free from the shackles of overthinking and embrace a mindset grounded in positivity and purpose.

We have explored various ways to nurture a motivational mindset essential for managing overthinking and to foster mental clarity. By integrating motivational content, you are equipped with a powerful tool to persist in your journey toward mental mastery. Remember, the stories and strategies shared here are not just theories but practical tools designed to inspire and guide you.

Positive thinking frameworks are your blueprint for building a resilient mind. These frameworks are more than just feel-good advice; they are structured approaches encouraging you to cultivate a proactive attitude toward your thought processes. Embrace these frameworks, apply them daily, and watch as your mindset transforms, enabling you to handle challenges easily and confidently.

The success stories we've discussed prove that effective thought management is achievable. These narratives are relatable and reinforce that you are not alone in this struggle. Each story echoes a journey of transformation possible for anyone, including you, provided commitment and the right strategies are in place.

Moving forward, I urge you to actively engage with these techniques. Apply the insights and strategies from this chapter consistently. Adjust them to fit your circumstances and reflect on your progress. This active engagement is crucial as it transforms theoretical knowledge into practical wisdom, cementing your path to overcoming overthinking.

You possess the inherent capability to master your thoughts and emotions. With each step you take using these strategies, you empower yourself to live a more focused and serene life. Let each success story remind you of the possibilities that await and motivate you to forge ahead with optimism and determination.

Remember, the journey to mental clarity is ongoing and requires perseverance. But with the right tools and a supportive framework, you are well-equipped to navigate this path successfully. Embrace these strategies, make them a part of your daily routine, and step confidently into a life characterized by enhanced mental clarity and reduced anxiety.

Chapter 14: A Relatable Guide to Rationality

Look past your thoughts so you may drink the

pure nectar of This Moment."

Rumi

Is Your Mind Playing Tricks on You? Discover the Path to Mental Mastery

Learning how to navigate the waters of our minds with precision and grace is essential in a world where our thoughts can often feel like an unstoppable torrent. This guide aims to equip you with the skills to steer clear of the whirlpools of overthinking and sail toward the serene seas of clarity and peace. Here, we dive deep into practical strategies that make sense and resonate deeply with your daily experiences, ensuring you're not just reading another self-help book but implementing a life-altering mindset.

As we approach the culmination of our journey together, this segment stands as a crucial pivot point, synthesizing all we have learned into actionable insights that promise to transform mental chaos into structured calm. It's about taking everything that has been absorbed and turning it into steps that are not only actionable but also sustainable.

Engagement through Relatability is key as we explore various anecdotes and sprinkle humor throughout our discussion. The aim is to paint a picture so vivid and relatable that you can see your thoughts and dilemmas mirrored in these scenarios. This approach makes learning enjoyable and cements these concepts in real-life contexts, making them easier to recall and apply when needed most.

A Conversational Tone helps in breaking down complex psychological barriers without overwhelming you. Think of it as having a heart-to-heart with a wise friend who understands your struggles and guides you through them with empathy and expertise. This tone encourages a two-way interaction, even through the pages of a book, allowing you to reflect actively on your thought processes and behaviors.

Lastly, ensuring Retention and Application of these strategies is paramount. By engaging in interactive elements such as reflective prompts or simple exercises, you are not just passively consuming content but actively integrating wisdom into your daily routines. Each strategy introduced is accompanied by a clear explanation of its importance and tips on how it can be seamlessly woven into your everyday life.

By now, it's clear that the battle against overthinking isn't fought on a single front. It's an amalgamation of understanding its roots, recognizing triggers, and consistently applying tailored strategies that resonate with personal experiences. Through cognitive-behavioral techniques and mindfulness practices detailed earlier in our discussions, this chapter aims to fortify your arsenal against anxiety and overthinking by focusing on practicality and personal growth.

The journey toward mental clarity is not about suppressing thoughts but understanding and redirecting them constructively. As you turn these pages, remember each step forward is a step away from the chaos of overthinking and towards the calmness of clear thinking.

Embrace these final insights with an open mind and an eager heart, ready to reclaim control over your mental landscape. Here lies not just the theory but the practice of achieving peace within one's mind—a practice that promises liberation from the incessant noise and a path towards profound personal fulfillment.

In rationality and mental clarity, relatability is crucial in engaging with the content effectively. We can bridge the gap between theory and practice by weaving anecdotes and humor into the fabric of the information presented, making it more relatable and enjoyable for readers. Picture this: you're faced with a challenging situation at work, feeling overwhelmed by the pressure to perform. Suddenly, a humorous story about a colleague's mishap lightens the mood and provides a fresh perspective on handling stress. Humor has a unique power to disarm tension and facilitate learning, creating a more receptive environment for new ideas to take root.

Anecdotes are real-life illustrations of abstract concepts, grounding them in tangible experiences that readers can easily grasp. Imagine reading about the benefits of mindfulness in reducing anxiety but then encountering a personal story about how practicing mindfulness helped someone navigate a difficult conversation with grace and composure. These narratives humanize the content, making it less intimidating and more relatable to our own lives.

Furthermore, humor acts as a catalyst for engagement, capturing attention and fostering a sense of camaraderie between the reader and the material. When complex ideas are delivered with levity, they become more digestible and memorable. Just like sharing a good laugh with a friend can strengthen your bond, injecting humor into educational content can enhance comprehension and retention.

In essence, utilizing anecdotes and humor is not just about entertainment; it's about creating an emotional connection with the material. When we feel connected to what we're learning, it becomes more meaningful and impactful. So, as we delve deeper into the world of rationality and mental clarity, remember that laughter is good for both the soul and the mind.

Embracing Mental Clarity

In mastering your mind and embracing mental clarity, connecting with experiences that resonate deeply is essential. Understanding that the challenges you face are shared by many can be a source of comfort and motivation on your journey toward a calmer state of mind. Acknowledging the universality of struggles with overthinking and anxiety helps you feel understood and less isolated in your battle against intrusive thoughts. It's crucial to realize that you are not alone in pursuing mental peace; many others have walked this path before you.

Finding relatable anecdotes and humor amid serious topics can lighten the emotional load and make the information more digestible. By weaving real-life stories into discussions about rationality and emotional mastery, the content becomes more engaging and easier to internalize. Humor can be a powerful tool in breaking down complex concepts into simpler, more approachable ideas. Embracing a conversational tone allows for a connection between the reader's personal experiences and the strategies presented, fostering camaraderie in exploring mental well-being.

Practical solutions that are easy to implement are pivotal in transforming knowledge into action. Simple, actionable advice empowers individuals to take control of their thoughts and emotions effectively. Encouraging readers to engage actively with strategies rather than passively absorbing information fosters a sense of agency and progress. Through practical steps and tangible results, true transformation occurs, leading to a deeper understanding of one's mental landscape.

Emphasizing the innate ability within each individual for emotional mastery is key to cultivating resilience and overcoming challenges. By highlighting our power to navigate our inner world with grace and strength, readers are inspired to tap into their potential for growth and self-improvement. The journey toward mental freedom begins with recognizing one's capacity for change and embracing it wholeheartedly. Through clear, concise language, readers are guided toward self-discovery and empowerment.

Incorporating relatable narratives, humor, and practical strategies enriches the learning experience. It ensures that the information is easily understood and applied in everyday life. By fostering a sense of connection through shared experiences and accessible advice, readers are encouraged to actively participate in their mental well-being journey. Remember, you hold the key to unlocking your mental clarity; it's time to embrace it with confidence and determination.

Applying Strategies for Lasting Mental Clarity

In this final part of the chapter, our goal is to ensure that the strategies and techniques discussed throughout the book are understood and actively applied in your daily life. It's essential to remember that knowledge without action yields minimal results. So, let's delve into how you can effectively retain and implement these valuable insights for your mental clarity journey.

Firstly, make a commitment to prioritize your mental well-being. This means setting aside dedicated time each day to practice the techniques outlined in the book. Whether it's mindfulness exercises, journaling, or positive affirmations, consistency is key to reaping the benefits of these practices.

Secondly, create a supportive environment that fosters your growth. Surround yourself with individuals who uplift and encourage you on your path to mental clarity. Share your goals with trusted friends or family members who can hold you accountable and provide motivation when needed.

Next, gradually integrate small changes into your routine rather than attempting a complete overhaul. Start with one technique and gradually incorporate others as you become more comfortable with them. This incremental approach increases the likelihood of long-term success.

Moreover, track your progress to stay motivated and celebrate your achievements. Keeping a journal or using an app to monitor your emotional state, thought patterns, and overall well-being can provide valuable insights into areas needing further attention.

Additionally, be patient with yourself as you navigate this journey towards mental clarity. Rome wasn't built in a day; similarly, lasting change takes time to manifest. Embrace setbacks as learning opportunities rather than viewing them as failures.

Furthermore, seek out additional resources or support if needed. Whether it's joining a mindfulness group, seeking therapy, or engaging with online communities focused on mental health, exploring different avenues of support can enhance your progress.

Lastly, remember that you possess the power within you to transform your thought patterns and embrace a calmer, more centered way of being. By implementing the strategies outlined in this book with dedication and perseverance, you are taking proactive steps toward unlocking the mental clarity you deserve.

Embrace this journey of self-discovery with an open mind and a willingness to challenge old habits. Your commitment to personal growth is commendable, and by actively engaging with these strategies, you are paving the way for a brighter, more fulfilling future filled with mental freedom and clarity.

This guide has explored how engaging storytelling, a conversational tone, and practical writing can transform complex psychological concepts into accessible and actionable knowledge. By infusing anecdotes and humor into our discussions, we've made the journey toward mental clarity not just educational but enjoyable. Remember, the effectiveness of what you've learned hinges on your willingness to apply these strategies consistently in daily life.

It's crucial to recognize the power of a relatable narrative. Stories make the content more engaging and help you see practical applications of cognitive-behavioral techniques in real-life scenarios. This approach ensures that the insights gained are theoretical, lived, and experienced, enhancing your ability to manage thoughts and emotions effectively.

We've tailored our discussions to resonate with your experiences, making the advice understandable and deeply personal. This personalized touch empowers you to implement changes confidently, knowing that the strategies discussed have been adapted to fit real, varied life contexts.

By fostering a dialogue rather than a monologue, we encourage you to actively participate in your journey toward mental clarity. Engagement is not merely about reading and understanding; it is about interacting with the content, questioning it, and molding it to fit your unique circumstances.

As we wrap up our exploration, remember that overcoming overthinking is ongoing. The tools and techniques shared here are designed for you to use and refine as you grow and as your circumstances evolve. The goal has always been to equip you with the knowledge to understand and disrupt the cycle of overthinking and anxiety, leading you toward a life characterized by greater calm and fulfillment.

Take these strategies, adapt them, and build on them. Your path to mental clarity is yours to shape. Armed with the right tools, each step forward can be confidently made. Embrace this journey with an open heart and a clear mind, ready to tackle the challenges ahead with newfound resilience.

This guide is more than just a collection of chapters; it is a toolkit for life. Each technique and advice is a component in your arsenal against overthinking and anxiety. Use them wisely, practice them regularly, and watch as your life transforms into clarity, purpose, and calm.

Epilogue

"The best way to capture moments is to pay attention.

This is how we cultivate mindfulness."

Jon Kabat-Zinn

Embracing the Horizon of Mental Clarity

As we conclude our journey together, we must reflect on the transformative insights and strategies we've explored. This book has been a guiding light towards understanding and mastering the complexities of your mind, providing you with the tools to overcome overthinking and embrace a life of clarity and calm.

The techniques and knowledge shared here are not just theoretical. Still, they are immensely applicable in everyday situations—whether at work, in personal relationships, or during moments of solitude. By integrating these practices into your daily life, you stand to gain peace of mind, enhanced decision-making abilities, and reduced anxiety.

We've delved deep into the causes of overthinking, uncovering its roots and triggers. We've explored cognitive-behavioral techniques that help reframe negative thinking patterns and mindfulness practices that encourage present-moment awareness. Remember, the power to change lies within your grasp; it's about consistently applying what you've learned.

To truly benefit from this book, it's crucial that you actively engage with the exercises provided, making them a part of your routine. Reflect on your progress regularly and adjust your strategies as needed. This is not a one-size-fits-all solution but a personalized journey toward mental wellness.

While this book provides a comprehensive guide to mastering your thoughts, it is important to acknowledge its limitations. Everyone is unique, and certain strategies might need adaptation to better suit different personal circumstances or deeper psychological issues requiring professional intervention.

I encourage you to view this not as an end but as the beginning of a lifelong practice. Continue exploring, learning, and adapting the most resonating strategies. Seek out further research if necessary, and remain open to new ways of enhancing your mental health.

As you move forward, remember that taking control of your thoughts is empowering. You can break free from the chains of overthinking that once held you back from experiencing life's full potential.

Final Thoughts

Let this book serve as a cornerstone for building a more mindful and fulfilled life. The path to mental clarity is ongoing—a journey that requires commitment, patience, and courage. Embrace each step confidently, knowing every effort brings you closer to a serene state of mind.

"The only limit to our realization of tomorrow

will be our doubts of today."

Franklin D. Roosevelt

Carry these words to remind you that your potential is boundless when freed from overthinking. Step boldly into each new day with clarity and purpose.

Conclusion

"In the end, just three things matter: How well

we have lived, how well we have loved,

how well we have learned to let go."

Jack Kornfield

Throughout this journey, you have explored various strategies and techniques to address and manage overthinking. By understanding the mechanics behind your thought patterns and recognizing the triggers that elevate your anxiety, you've taken crucial steps towards regaining control over your mental well-being. Remember, awareness is the key to change. It is the first and most significant step in transforming your life.

Embracing cognitive-behavioral techniques has given you tools to reshape your mindset, challenge irrational beliefs, and reframe negative thoughts. These strategies empower you to view your experiences through a more balanced and realistic lens. As you continue to practice these techniques, they will become an integral part of your daily routine, fostering a healthier, more positive way of thinking.

Mindfulness practices have also played a pivotal role in guiding you toward a more centered and peaceful state of being. By learning to stay present and engage fully with the current moment, you've reduced the tendency to get lost in endless cycles of overthinking. Cultivating mindfulness allows you to experience life more deeply and authentically, enhancing your connection with yourself and the world around you.

One of the essential takeaways from this book is the power of personal and shared narratives. The stories and anecdotes woven throughout these chapters illustrate the concepts' applicability. They also remind you that you are not alone in your struggles; many others are on a similar path toward mental clarity and freedom from overthinking.

Your journey is unique, and the ability to personalize and adapt the strategies presented is crucial for lasting transformation. Reflect on your experiences, apply the techniques in ways that resonate with you, and make the practices your own. The interactive exercises and reflections are designed to deepen your engagement and facilitate meaningful change.

It's vital to approach this journey with patience and self-compassion. Progress is not always linear, and there will be moments of challenge and clarity. The important thing is to persist and remain gentle with yourself. Remember that change takes time, and you will achieve lasting transformation with consistent effort.

As you continue on this path, here are a few key points to keep in mind:

- Stay aware of your triggers: Identifying what prompts your overthinking can help you prevent or manage episodes more effectively.
- Use cognitive-behavioral techniques daily: Reframe negative thoughts and challenge irrational beliefs regularly to reinforce positive thinking patterns.
- Practice mindfulness: Engage in mindfulness exercises regularly to remain present and reduce stress.
- Reflect on your progress: Review your journey and acknowledge your achievements. Celebrate the small victories.
- Be patient and compassionate with yourself: Recognize that lasting change is a gradual process, and be kind to yourself throughout it.

Integrating these practices into your life sets the foundation for a more mindful, balanced, and fulfilling existence. The journey towards mental clarity is ongoing, but with perseverance and confidence, you are well-equipped to navigate the challenges ahead and embrace the richness of life without the burden of overthinking.

Bonus Material

Your Questions, Answered!

1. How do I know if my overthinking is severe enough to warrant using these techniques?

Determining the severity of your overthinking can often be challenging, as it may present itself in various forms and intensities. Generally, overthinking becomes a concern when it significantly impacts your daily life. This can manifest as constant rumination or replaying events in your mind to the extent that it interferes with your ability to concentrate, make decisions, or sleep. Suppose you find yourself frequently stuck in cycles of worry or excessive contemplation that prevent you from moving forward. In that case, it indicates that intervention is required.

One major factor to consider is the emotional toll that overthinking takes on you. Suppose you are consistently feeling overwhelmed, anxious, or depressed due to your thought patterns. In that case, these are strong signs that your overthinking is severe. Emotional distress triggered by constant mental rumination can hinder your ability to enjoy life, maintain healthy relationships, and perform effectively at work or school. The cognitive-behavioral techniques and mindfulness practices discussed in the book can be powerful tools to mitigate these negative emotions and restore balance and control.

Another indicator is the impact of overthinking on your physical health. Chronic stress from overthinking can lead to physical symptoms such as headaches, muscle tension, and stomach problems. You might also experience fatigue due to the mental exhaustion of constantly overanalyzing situations. Suppose your physical health is suffering as a result of your thought patterns. In that case, applying the techniques outlined in this book to manage and reduce your overthinking is even more critical.

Lastly, assess how much overthinking affects your decision-making and problem-solving abilities. Severe overthinking can lead to analysis paralysis, where you become so caught up in the details and potential outcomes that you cannot make any decisions. This can stall personal and professional progress. Using the techniques provided, you can learn to break down problems into manageable chunks, challenge irrational beliefs, and ultimately arrive at decisions with greater confidence and clarity.

In summary, if overthinking substantially disrupts your daily life, emotional well-being, physical health, or decision-making abilities, it is severe enough to warrant using cognitive-behavioral techniques, mindfulness practices, and other strategies discussed in this book. Recognizing the severity of your overthinking is the first step towards taking proactive measures to manage it effectively and regain control over your mental and emotional health.

2. Can cognitive-behavioral techniques be effective if my anxiety is situational or sporadic rather than chronic?

Absolutely. Cognitive-behavioral techniques (CBT) can be highly effective for managing situational or sporadic anxiety as well as chronic cases. The principles of CBT focus on identifying and challenging irrational thoughts and beliefs, which can be beneficial regardless of the frequency or intensity of your anxiety. By applying CBT practices, you can develop healthier thought patterns and coping mechanisms that enable you to handle anxiety-provoking situations more effectively.

For situational anxiety, such as anxiety triggered by specific events like public speaking or social interactions, CBT can help you reframe negative thoughts and reduce the impact of these episodes. Techniques like cognitive restructuring, exposure therapy, and relaxation strategies can equip you with practical tools to face your fears and diminish their hold on you.

Even if your anxiety is not a constant presence, the skills you honed through CBT can still be invaluable. These techniques prepare you to cope with future stressors and prevent episodic anxiety from escalating or recurring. Remember, the occasional use of CBT methods can be just as transformative as a regimen designed for chronic anxiety. Integrating these practices into daily life can enhance mental resilience and overall well-being.

3. After starting these practices, how long does it typically take to notice a significant change in my thought patterns?

The time it takes to notice a significant change in your thought patterns after starting cognitive-behavioral techniques and mindfulness practices can vary greatly from person to person. Generally, many individuals see noticeable improvements within a few weeks to a couple of months of consistent practice. Factors such as the frequency and intensity of the practices, individual differences in psychological resilience, and the specific nature of one's thought patterns all play a role in determining the timeline for change.

For some, the initial stages of implementing these practices may feel challenging, as old thought patterns are deeply ingrained and resistant to change. However, with persistence and regular application, these techniques rewire the brain's cognitive processes over time. Maintaining a positive outlook and not becoming discouraged if progress seems slow at first is important. Remember that developing new mental habits is a gradual process, and small, incremental changes build up to create substantial improvement over time.

Measuring progress can also be subjective, as changes in thought patterns might initially manifest in subtle ways. You might notice that you are less reactive to stressors, more present in your daily activities, or able to challenge negative thoughts more effectively. Keeping a journal to track your thoughts and emotions can be a helpful tool in recognizing and appreciating the progress you are making, even if it feels slow.

Ultimately, the key to achieving and maintaining significant change lies in these techniques' consistent and dedicated practice. The more you commit to integrating cognitive-behavioral techniques and mindfulness into your daily routine, the more you will experience their cumulative benefits. Patience and persistence are crucial, as the journey to transforming your thought patterns and improving your mental well-being is a long-term investment in your overall quality of life.

4. Are there specific mindfulness exercises recommended for beginners to avoid feeling overwhelmed?

Absolutely. For beginners, starting with simple and manageable mindfulness exercises can greatly help avoid feeling overwhelmed. One foundational exercise is mindful breathing. This practice involves focusing purely on the breath, noticing each inhale and exhale without attempting to change the natural rhythm of breathing. By centering attention on the breath, beginners can cultivate a sense of calm and present moment awareness, making it an excellent entry point into mindfulness.

Another beginner-friendly exercise is the body scan. This technique involves slowly shifting attention through different body parts, from the toes to the head, and noticing any sensations, tensions, or relaxation areas. The body scan encourages a non-judgmental awareness of physical sensations and helps ground the individual in the present moment. This method is useful for developing a greater connection between the mind and body. It can be a relaxing way to ease into mindfulness practice.

Mindful walking is also a recommended exercise for those new to mindfulness. This involves paying close attention to the physical act of walking, noticing the sensations in the feet, the movement of the legs, and the engagement of muscles. Individuals can foster a deeper sense of presence and tranquility by focusing on each step. Combining mindfulness with gentle physical activity can be particularly effective for those who find sitting still challenging.

Lastly, engaging in short gratitude practices can be beneficial for beginners. This exercise entails reflecting on and mentally listing things one is grateful for, which can shift focus from negative thoughts to positive ones. A few minutes each day dedicated to recognizing gratitude can enhance overall well-being and help cultivate a mindful, appreciative mindset. When practiced consistently, these exercises can serve as the building blocks for a robust and sustainable mindfulness routine.

5. What should I do if I find it challenging to identify my triggers for overthinking?

Identifying triggers for overthinking can be challenging, especially when these triggers are subtle or deeply ingrained in daily habits. A structured approach to uncovering these triggers begins with self-awareness and active reflection. Start by keeping a dedicated journal where you note instances of intense overthinking. Write down the context, thoughts, emotions, and preceding events. Over time, patterns may emerge that reveal specific situations, people, or activities that regularly lead to overthinking.

Another effective method is to engage in mindfulness practices, which can provide clarity and heightened awareness of your internal states. Practicing mindfulness makes you more attuned to your thoughts and emotions in real time. This heightened awareness can help you identify the onset of overthinking more quickly and understand the circumstances that trigger it. Mindfulness meditation, for instance, encourages you to observe your thoughts without judgment, which can reveal the underlying triggers fueling your overthinking.

Additionally, considering external feedback can be immensely beneficial. Sometimes, those close to you might notice patterns you might not see in your behavior. Seeking input from trusted friends, family members, or a therapist can provide new perspectives on what might trigger your overthinking. This external viewpoint can often illuminate triggers that are not immediately obvious.

Finally, cognitive-behavioral techniques can also be instrumental in identifying and addressing overthinking triggers. CBT encourages you to challenge and reframe negative thought patterns by understanding the connections between thoughts, emotions, and behaviors. By systematically examining these relationships, you can identify specific triggers and develop strategies to mitigate their impact. Working with a CBT practitioner can provide structure and support as you navigate this process, helping ensure you can effectively manage and reduce overthinking.

6. Can these strategies be integrated into a busy daily routine, and if so, how?

Certainly, integrating cognitive-behavioral techniques and mindfulness into a busy daily routine requires purposeful planning and dedication. One effective approach is to start with micro-practices, or small, manageable units of mindfulness or cognitive exercises that fit seamlessly into your day. This can be as simple as dedicating five minutes in the morning to mindful breathing or a short body scan before bed. These brief practices can provide significant benefits and are less likely to be skipped due to time constraints.

Furthermore, incorporating mindfulness into daily activities is another practical method. For example, you can practice mindfulness while commuting by paying attention to the sensations of driving or riding, the sounds around you, and the environment. Even mundane tasks like washing dishes or taking a shower can be transformed into mindfulness exercises by focusing on the sensory experiences associated with these activities. This approach ensures that mindfulness becomes integral to your routine without requiring additional time.

Setting reminders throughout the day can also be helpful. These reminders can prompt you to take a few moments to check in with yourself, take deep breaths, and observe your thoughts and feelings non-judgmentally. Technology, such as mindfulness apps or even setting alarms on your phone, can assist in maintaining regular practice. Consistently responding to these prompts helps establish mindfulness as a habitual part of your day.

To address cognitive-behavioral techniques, integrating them into daily life can be smoothly accomplished by associating them with triggering events as they arise. For instance, if you notice negative thinking patterns during certain tasks or interactions, take a moment to challenge those thoughts right then and there. Utilize brief but effective CBT strategies, such as cognitive restructuring, to examine and reframe unhelpful thoughts into more balanced perspectives. This on-the-spot application encourages practice and reinforces these techniques as part of your coping toolkit.

Ultimately, patience and persistence form the cornerstone of integrating these practices into a busy lifestyle. It's essential to remember that both mindfulness and cognitive-behavioral approaches are skills that develop over time. Gradual, consistent incorporation, coupled with a forgiving attitude towards setbacks, ensures steady progress and underscores the long-term investment in mental well-being. The ongoing commitment promises cumulative benefits and enriches your overall quality of life, making the effort worthwhile.

7. How can I stay motivated to consistently apply these techniques, especially during harder times?

Staying motivated to consistently apply mindfulness and cognitive-behavioral techniques, especially during harder times, requires a multifaceted approach rooted in understanding, self-compassion, and strategic planning. One of the key aspects is to establish clear, personal reasons for why these practices are important to you. Reflecting on the benefits of routine practice, such as reduced anxiety, improved focus, and enhanced emotional balance, can reinforce your commitment. It can be helpful to write down these benefits and place them somewhere visible as a constant reminder of these techniques' positive impact on your life.

Another crucial factor in maintaining motivation is to set realistic and achievable goals. Break down your larger objectives into smaller, more manageable steps. For instance, if you want to practice mindfulness for 20 minutes daily, start with 5 minutes and gradually increase the duration. Similarly, with cognitive-behavioral techniques, one specific strategy should be selected to focus on initially rather than trying to master multiple techniques at once. Celebrating small victories along the way can boost your morale and demonstrate progress, making the overall goal feel more attainable.

Building a supportive environment is also instrumental in staying motivated. Engaging with a community, such as a mindfulness group or therapy session, provides a sense of accountability and shared experience. Discussing your challenges and successes with others on a similar journey can offer encouragement and practical advice. Additionally, talking with a trusted friend, family member, or a professional can provide external reinforcement and support during difficult times when your personal motivation might wane.

Lastly, practicing self-compassion is essential when navigating harder times. Recognize that setbacks are a normal part of any journey, and don't equate them with failure. Instead, view them as opportunities to learn and grow. When you experience slumps in motivation, be kind to yourself and avoid self-criticism. Reframe your approach to see each day as a new opportunity to practice mindfulness and cognitive-behavioral techniques, irrespective of the previously mentioned challenges. This helps build resilience and ensures you remain committed to your path towards mental well-being, even during the most challenging periods.

8. Is it beneficial to seek professional help or therapy with the practices mentioned in the book?

Seeking professional help or therapy alongside practicing mindfulness and cognitive-behavioral techniques can be immensely beneficial, and the reasons are multifaceted. Firstly, professionals such as therapists or counselors come equipped with specialized training and knowledge that enable them to provide personalized guidance tailored to your unique needs and circumstances. Through a professional's insight, you can better understand your mental health challenges and develop a more effective strategy for integrating these techniques into your daily life. They can help identify specific triggers, patterns, and obstacles you might not have noticed, ensuring a more targeted and efficient approach to your mental well-being.

Moreover, professional help provides a structured environment for learning and practicing new skills. Those new to mindfulness or cognitive-behavioral techniques often benefit from the structured setting that therapy can offer, making it easier to understand and apply these practices. During therapy sessions, you can receive immediate feedback and monitor your progress, allowing for the timely adjustment of your techniques if needed. A therapist can also offer strategies and tools beyond basic mindfulness and CBT approaches, enhancing your coping mechanisms' overall breadth and depth.

Additionally, the accountability that comes with professional therapy is a significant motivator for many. Knowing that you have regular sessions encourages a more consistent practice, as you are likely more committed to your routine when you know you will discuss your progress with a therapist. This external accountability can be crucial, especially during tougher times when your motivation might be low. The therapeutic relationship offers emotional support and validation, which are essential for maintaining morale and determination.

Finally, professional help complements self-guided practices by providing a comprehensive and holistic approach to mental health. While self-practice can be incredibly empowering, it must often be more coordinated to effectively address deeper or more complex issues. A therapist can help you integrate these practices into a broader treatment plan, addressing underlying concerns such as trauma, anxiety, or depression, which might be beyond the scope of self-practice alone. This integration ensures you practice mindfulness and cognitive-behavioral techniques within a supportive and well-rounded framework that promotes sustained mental health and well-being.

9. How do I handle setbacks or times when I feel like I'm regressing in my progress?

Handling setbacks or times when you feel you're progressing can be challenging. Still, it's an integral part of any journey toward mental well-being. Setbacks are common and can occur for various reasons, such as increased stress, significant life changes, or simply the natural ebb and flow of motivation and energy. It's crucial to approach these periods with a mindset of growth and resilience rather than self-criticism. Understanding that setbacks are not a reflection of your abilities or worth but rather an opportunity for learning and development can help you navigate these times more effectively.

One fundamental strategy is to re-evaluate your goals and current practices. Often, setbacks occur because your existing strategies no longer align with your present circumstances or needs. Take a step back and assess whether your goals are still realistic and achievable. Consider if new stressors or challenges in your life require an adjustment in your approach. It may be helpful to break down your goals into smaller, more manageable tasks and focus on making incremental progress. For example, if you find it difficult to maintain a daily mindfulness practice, try reducing the time commitment or incorporating mindfulness techniques into everyday activities like walking or eating.

Building a support network is another vital component in managing setbacks. Whether through professional help, therapy, or personal connections, having people to turn to can provide the encouragement and accountability needed to persevere. Discussing your experiences with someone who understands your journey can offer new perspectives and practical advice. Additionally, joining a support group where others share similar challenges can foster a sense of community and shared purpose, which can be incredibly reassuring during regression times.

It's also essential to cultivate self-compassion and practice self-care. When faced with setbacks, it's easy to fall into a cycle of negative self-talk and blame. However, being kind to yourself and recognizing that setbacks are a normal part of any improvement process can mitigate this. Engage in activities that promote relaxation and well-being, such as exercise, hobbies, or spending time with loved ones. Taking care of your physical health through proper nutrition and sleep can reinforce your resilience and improve your ability to cope with challenges.

Maintaining a reflective practice can help you understand and learn from setbacks. Journaling your thoughts, feelings, and experiences can offer insights into what might be contributing to your regression and how you can address these issues moving forward. Reflect on past successes and challenges to identify patterns and strategies that worked before. This practice not only aids in personal growth but also helps track your progress over time, reminding you that setbacks do not erase your progress. Combining reflection, support, and self-compassion allows you to navigate setbacks more effectively and continue your journey toward mental well-being.

10.   Are there particular life situations where these techniques may not be effective or need adapting?

In particular life situations, mindfulness and cognitive-behavioral techniques may not be as effective or require adaptation. For instance, these practices may not provide immediate relief in situations involving acute crises or trauma. Experiencing a traumatic event can trigger a wide range of intense emotions and physical responses that may overwhelm an individual's capacity to utilize mindfulness and CBT effectively at the moment. In such cases, immediate intervention from a mental health professional or emergency services may be necessary before these techniques can be beneficially applied.

Furthermore, individuals facing severe mental health disorders like major depressive disorder, generalized anxiety disorder, or post-traumatic stress disorder (PTSD) may find that mindfulness and CBT alone are insufficient as a primary form of treatment. While these methods can certainly complement medical treatments, including medication and more intensive therapeutic interventions, they may need to be adapted to fit the individual's specific needs and symptoms. For example, a person with severe depression might experience cognitive distortions that make traditional CBT challenging; in such cases, a therapist might modify the approach or incorporate additional strategies to ensure it's effective.

Another life situation where these techniques might need adapting is during significant life changes or transitions, such as divorce, job loss, or the death of a loved one. The emotional upheaval and stress associated with these events can make it difficult to remain consistent with self-practice. Adapting the techniques to be more flexible and context-appropriate can help maintain their effectiveness. For instance, focusing on simple mindfulness exercises that promote grounding and presence might be more beneficial during overwhelming grief than rigorous cognitive restructuring exercises.

Moreover, sociocultural factors can also play a role in the effectiveness of mindfulness and CBT. Cultural background, belief systems, and societal norms can influence an individual's comfort level with these techniques. For example, someone from a culture that stigmatizes mental health issues might initially struggle with self-acceptance practices central to mindfulness. Similarly, cognitive-behavioral approaches emphasizing individualism could be less effective in cultures prioritizing community and collective well-being. In such scenarios, therapists might need to integrate culturally sensitive approaches or adapt the techniques to align more closely with the individual's cultural context.

Lastly, certain physical health conditions can impact the applicability of mindfulness and CBT. Chronic pain, for example, requires specific mindfulness techniques that focus on pain management and acceptance rather than stress reduction alone. Adapting the practice to accommodate physical limitations and addressing specific health concerns through a tailored approach can enhance the effectiveness of these techniques. While mindfulness and CBT are versatile and powerful tools, their application must be mindful of the individual's context, health status, and cultural background to ensure that they provide the intended benefits.

11. Can the exercises and reflections in the book be done collaboratively with a partner or a friend?

The exercises and reflections in the book can be done collaboratively with a partner or a friend, providing numerous advantages. Engaging in these practices with someone else can foster a greater sense of accountability and motivation. You will likely stay committed to the practice when you share your goals and experiences with others. Moreover, a partner can offer encouragement and support during challenging moments, making it easier to persist through tough times. This collaboration can transform solitary exercises into shared activities, enhancing the overall learning and growth experience.

Collaboratively doing these exercises can also lead to deeper insights and more comprehensive reflections. When two individuals discuss their thoughts and experiences, they can provide diverse perspectives that enrich the understanding of the concepts. This dialogue allows individuals to see beyond their subjective experiences and consider different viewpoints, which can be particularly beneficial in cognitive-behavioral techniques. For example, a friend might help identify cognitive distortions that one might overlook or offer alternative interpretations that facilitate cognitive restructuring.

In addition to cognitive benefits, practicing these exercises with a partner can strengthen social bonds and foster a sense of community. Shared experiences often lead to stronger connections, creating open communication and emotional support opportunities. This can be incredibly valuable in enhancing emotional resilience, as knowing someone else is experiencing similar challenges can alleviate feelings of isolation. The mutual support and empathy developed from this collaborative approach can improve the mental well-being of both parties involved.

However, it's important to note that collaboration should be approached mindfully to ensure it remains productive and supportive. Each participant should respect the other's boundaries and be willing to communicate honestly and openly. Finding a partner equally committed to the practice is vital to maintaining balance and avoiding dependency. Establishing clear expectations and being open to adjusting the approach as needed can help ensure that the collaborative experience remains beneficial and aligned with the individual goals of both participants.

These exercises and reflections with a partner or friend can enhance accountability, deepen understanding, and build stronger emotional connections. By navigating the journey together, individuals may find greater success and fulfillment in their pursuit of mental well-being.

12. How do I balance being present and engaged in the moment with planning and preparing for the future?

Balancing being present and engaged at the moment with planning and preparing for the future can often seem like a challenging duality to manage. This balance requires an understanding that living fully in the present does not negate the value of foresight and preparation. Rather, it involves integrating mindfulness with a structured approach to future planning. Mindfulness teaches us to anchor ourselves in the current experience and to fully appreciate and engage with our emotions, sensations, and environment. By being present, we can reduce anxiety and stress that often stem from overthinking the future or ruminating over the past.

Setting aside dedicated time for future planning is crucial to achieving this balance. Engage in periods of focused planning where you outline goals, establish action plans, and identify potential challenges. During these sessions, allow yourself to think comprehensively about your future without the guilt of feeling detached from the present. Once these future goals are articulated and a plan is in place, you can return to the present with a clearer mind and a sense of direction. This structured planning ensures that while you are mindfully present, a roadmap guides your forward movement.

Adopting a flexible mindset is another key to balancing the present with future planning. Recognize that plans may need to adapt to changing circumstances and new information. Flexibility allows you to adjust your plans without feeling unmoored or overly stressed about deviations. Flexibility also means appreciating the process and progress rather than fixating solely on outcomes. As you become more adept at being present, you'll cultivate a stronger resilience to unexpected changes, viewing them as opportunities rather than setbacks.

Furthermore, integrating mindfulness practices into your daily routine can enhance this balance. Mindfulness exercises such as meditation, deep-breathing techniques, and mindful journaling can help ground you in the present moment. These practices enhance your awareness and appreciation of the current moment, making it easier to release future anxieties and past regrets. At the same time, they can improve your focus and clarity when it comes time to engage in future planning, ultimately creating a harmonious synergy between living presently and preparing for what's ahead.

Lastly, being present can actually enhance your ability to plan effectively. When fully engaged in the present moment, you develop a more profound awareness of your values, preferences, and priorities. These insights are invaluable when making informed decisions about your future. By understanding and connecting with yourself deeper, you ensure that your future plans are aligned with your true self, leading to more fulfilling and authentic goals. Balancing present mindfulness with future planning is about embracing a holistic way of living that honors both the now and the not yet, creating a more centered, proactive, and serene life.

13. What role do physical health and wellness play in managing overthinking, and are there any specific recommendations?

Physical health and wellness play a pivotal role in managing overthinking as a preventative measure and an active intervention. When the body is in optimal health, the mind is better equipped to handle stressors, reducing the propensity to overthink. Regular physical activity, in particular, has been shown to release endorphins and other neurochemicals that promote a sense of well-being and mental clarity. This creates a positive feedback loop: enhanced physical health improves mental resilience, reducing the likelihood of getting caught in cycles of rumination and anxiety.

Exercise can also serve as a form of meditation in motion. Activities such as running, swimming, or yoga require a form of mental engagement that redirects focus away from negative thought patterns and towards the task at hand. This breaks the cycle of overthinking and cultivates a habit of attentiveness and presence that can be carried over into daily life. Moreover, the physical fatigue that comes from consistent exercise can enhance sleep quality, which is crucial for cognitive function and emotional regulation. Poor sleep often exacerbates overthinking and anxiety, creating a vicious cycle that impacts both mental and physical health.

Beyond exercise, nutrition plays a significant role in mental well-being. A well-balanced diet rich in essential nutrients supports brain function and emotional stability. For instance, omega-3 fatty acids in fish, flaxseed, and walnuts support cognitive health. Vitamins such as B12 and D, as well as minerals like magnesium, have been linked to reduced symptoms of anxiety and depression. Hydration is equally important, as even mild dehydration can affect mood, energy levels, and cognitive abilities. One can lay a solid foundation for a healthier mind by fuelling the body with the right nutrients.

Additionally, engaging in wellness practices such as mindfulness, meditation, and breathwork can further bolster one's ability to manage overthinking. These practices train the brain to focus on the present moment, making it easier to let go of intrusive thoughts and anxieties about the future. Techniques like deep breathing and progressive muscle relaxation activate the parasympathetic nervous system, inducing a state of calm that makes it easier to approach problems with a clear and balanced mind. Over time, these practices can rewire neural pathways, making it easier to manage stress and break the habit of overthinking.

Lastly, a supportive community and healthy social interactions should not be overlooked. Group sports, fitness classes, or even regular walks with friends can provide physical exercise and social support. Interacting with others can offer new perspectives and solutions that might not be readily apparent when stuck in their own head. Emotional support from friends and loved ones can alleviate feelings of isolation, making it easier to manage stress and overthinking. Ultimately, a holistic approach integrating physical health, nutrition, mindfulness, and social support offers the most robust framework for tackling overthinking and fostering overall mental wellness.

14.   Can the power of narrative and storytelling be used in other areas of personal development outside of overthinking?

Yes, the power of narrative and storytelling can be instrumental in various areas of personal development beyond just managing to overthink. At its core, storytelling is a fundamental way humans make sense of the world and their place in it. It can be a potent tool for self-reflection, helping individuals to understand their past experiences and how those experiences have shaped their beliefs, emotions, and behaviors. When one crafts a personal narrative, they are curating their life's story, focusing on certain events, challenges, and triumphs. This active engagement in creating one's narrative can foster a greater sense of agency and empowerment, enabling individuals to reframe negative experiences in a more constructive light.

In goal setting and achievement, storytelling can serve as a motivational tool. By envisioning future success as a narrative, one can create a detailed and vivid picture of desired outcomes, making abstract goals more tangible and attainable. This method, often called "visioning," encourages individuals to script a narrative where they have already achieved their goals. Such detailed visualization can bolster confidence and persistence as the brain perceives these imagined accomplishments as feasible targets rather than distant aspirations. This powerful narrative technique can be immensely helpful in both personal and professional contexts, aiding in pursuing long-term goals and ambitions.

Storytelling also plays a crucial role in emotional healing and personal growth. Through therapeutic practices like journaling or sharing one's experiences in support groups, individuals can process traumas and difficult emotions by framing them coherently. This process, known as narrative therapy, allows individuals to externalize their issues, thereby gaining new perspectives and insights. By reauthoring their stories, people can shift from viewing themselves as victims of their circumstances to seeing themselves as resilient survivors who have overcome significant challenges. This reframe not only aids in healing but also in developing a more resilient and positive self-identity.

Moreover, storytelling can enhance communication skills and foster better relationships. Crafting and sharing personal stories require vulnerability and openness, which can create deeper emotional connections with others. When individuals share their narratives, it invites empathy and understanding, breaking down barriers and building trust. In professional settings, storytelling can be a powerful way to influence and inspire, making complex ideas more relatable and memorable. Leaders who effectively use storytelling can foster a shared vision, mobilize teams, and drive organizational change by connecting to their audience on a human level.

In summary, the power of narrative and storytelling extends far beyond managing overthinking. It is a versatile tool that can aid in self-reflection, goal attainment, emotional healing, and effective communication. By engaging with and crafting our own stories, we gain a deeper understanding of ourselves and our experiences, enhancing various facets of personal development and enriching our interactions with others.

15.   How do I create a supportive environment that encourages the continued practice of mindfulness and cognitive-behavioral techniques?

Creating a supportive environment that encourages the continued practice of mindfulness and cognitive-behavioral techniques (CBT) involves several key elements, each contributing to a cohesive and nurturing space where individuals feel motivated and capable of sustaining their mental wellness practices. Firstly, it is essential to cultivate a physical space conducive to mindfulness. This might include a quiet and uncluttered area dedicated to meditation or relaxation, equipped with comfortable seating, soft lighting, and calming elements like plants or artwork. Such an environment can help signal to the brain that it is time to focus inward and be present, making it easier to transition into a mindful state.

Beyond the physical setup, fostering a culture of mindfulness within a community or household can significantly enhance commitment to these practices. This can be achieved by setting collective intentions, such as scheduling regular group meditation sessions or mindfulness workshops. Encouraging open discussions about the benefits and challenges of these practices can also help normalize mindfulness and CBT as integral parts of daily life. Moreover, integrating mindfulness into routine activities, like mindful eating or mindful walking, ensures that these practices become a natural and seamless part of one's lifestyle rather than an isolated activity.

Supportive social interactions play a crucial role in maintaining mindfulness and CBT practices. Participating in group settings, such as meditation circles, CBT groups, or online communities, can provide a sense of belonging and accountability. Sharing experiences with others on similar journeys can offer new insights, encouragement, and the motivation to stay committed. Also, it is vital to foster an environment where individuals feel safe to express their thoughts and experiences without judgment. This emotional safety can enhance one's willingness to engage deeply with mindfulness and CBT techniques, knowing they are supported and understood.

Lastly, ongoing education and resources are fundamental to

sustaining the practice of mindfulness and CBT. Access to books, guided meditations, workshops, and even apps can provide continuous learning and inspiration. Having expert speakers or instructors for regular sessions can also reinvigorate interest and provide deeper knowledge and skills. By prioritizing a supportive, educated, and engaged community, it is feasible to maintain an environment that encourages and thrives on the continued practice of mindfulness and cognitive-behavioral techniques.

Thank You

We sincerely appreciate you taking the time to read this book. Your commitment to self-improvement and mindfulness is commendable, and we are honored to have been a part of your journey.

We hope these pages' insights and techniques inspire you to cultivate a more balanced, mindful, and fulfilling life. Remember, every step you take towards bettering yourself makes a significant difference.

Thank you for allowing us to accompany you on this personal growth and transformation path.